IN THE NICK OF TIME

Palmetto Publishing Group
Charleston, SC

In the Nick of Time

First Edition

Printed in the United States

ISBN-13: 978-1-64111-724-1
ISBN-10: 1-64111-724-9

IN THE NICK OF TIME

Rising to Resilience from the Depths of Betrayal

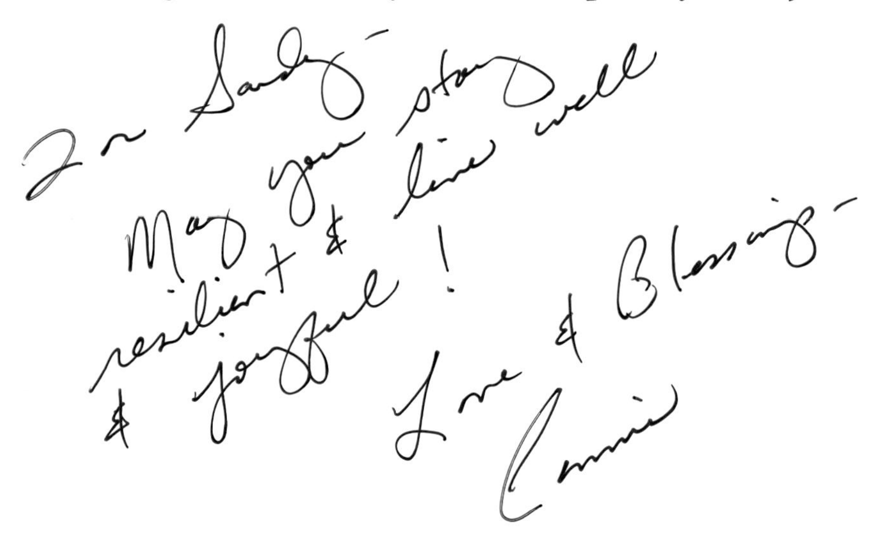

Constance Clancy, Ed.D.

Foreword

By Dr. Anne Brown, RNCS
Author of *Backbone Power: The Science of Saying No*

Whenever I ask my Twitter followers the questions:

1. What do you want me to write about?
2. What area of your emotional health is giving you challenges?

The answer is usually requesting help with recovering from the emotional damage of being with a partner who has the diagnosis of Narcissistic Personality Disorder (NPD). Many people also ask how to leave when you discover your partner has NPD or how to deal with a family member who has married someone with NPD. We are living during a time when, for many reasons, people with NPD are enabled, alive, and well. We see people with NPD in many places including, but not limited to, our government, the top 1%, people driven by power and greed, the heads of corporations, and our own little worlds. Unfortunately, as a society we have inadvertently and unknowingly enabled those with NPD.

I strongly believe that knowledge empowers us. We don't know what we don't know until our blindness is revealed to us. In order to stop enabling people who will primarily put themselves first and at the expense of others, we need knowledge. We need to have our blindness revealed to us.

When someone who is already in a helping profession meets a challenge such as a marriage to someone with NPD, it is generally to enrich her or his journey. She or he will then use the experience and knowledge gained to lead others out of their pain and suffering.

Constance wanted to write this book to help others understand these types of relationships, learn how to heal from them, and then rise to joy and resilience. No one needs to stay in a toxic relationship. You can get out and learn to really be committed to "No Contact." There is help. This book is educational and healing for those who are being or have been victimized by toxicity.

One can not only survive narcissistic abuse, but also thrive. Constance gives you guidelines to live healthier and happier with joy and resilience.

Constance has the tools and techniques to assist with healing and embrace resilience. She believes that through hypnotherapy, deprogramming of negative beliefs, and reprogramming of positive beliefs in one's subconscious mind, one can begin a strong, healing journey. Healing starts from within, and hypnotherapy can be a powerful tool when combined with talk therapy. Accessing the subconscious mind, which operates 95% of the time, is crucial to releasing the deep wounding over time that has occurred.

Constance did her own counseling and healing through self-hypnosis, Eye Movement Desensitization and Reprocessing (EMDR), and talk therapy. As you read this book, you will come to understand how these three modalities helped her successfully heal from her toxic marriage. You will also gain an understanding of ways for you to heal, thrive, and finally be independent and free.

INTRODUCTION

As a practicing holistic psychotherapist for 30 years, I have worked with many people from all walks of life and from all over the world. I have found that we are very similar in nature, experiencing many commonalities and heartfelt challenges and concerns for ourselves and others. I have specialized in providing guidance and healthy coping techniques for their trauma, heartbreak, abandonment, betrayal, grief, and healing.

Although we all have our challenges, nothing quite prepared me for marriage, the biggest challenge and lesson of my life thus far.

Over the past few years, I have been reading, researching, and coming to grips with understanding the spectrum of empaths and narcissists while healing from the depths of betrayal from my first and only marriage. I know a lot more now than I did when I filed for divorce in March 2017. I had only been married for six years. Short-term marriage, the attorneys called it. My focus consisted of the emotional and physical affairs he was having, why he abandoned me, and my feelings of betrayal. How could someone who professed his love for me and asked me to marry him betray me? It didn't make sense at the time. I knew I had to explore what inside of me lost myself and married someone who lived a lie. I had to turn to my own dark night of the soul. Seeking solitude, diving deep into my own spiritual practice, seeking a trusted therapist, reprogramming my own subconscious beliefs, and being in nature were all important and necessary components to my healing.

If you have been through deception and experienced betrayal, a breach of trust, you know. Betrayal is a pain you cannot quite fathom until it happens to you. Betrayal brings loss, ranging from mini losses to life-shattering losses that make you question if you will ever be the same. With willingness and desire, you can not only heal and survive, but also rise to resilience and thrive.

I have heard that it takes two to five years to heal from betrayal in an intimate relationship. I do believe when one is betrayed early on in life, there is a susceptibility to re-experience betrayal later in life. The trigger of the original betrayal surfaces and you are faced with triggers of the original betrayal all over again because that early trauma was locked inside of you, and if you didn't work through it, it never went away. Every loss is individual, and the grief process varies for everyone. I was determined not to give away any more power. Three years later, I am resilient, giving seminars on the topic of empaths and narcissists, rising to resilience from the depths of betrayal, and feeling as though my life is whole and balanced again. I'm not saying that the pain doesn't resurface at times, especially as I write about some painful experiences, but overall, I am one of the fortunate ones, happier than ever and, call it what you will—the inner gift of wisdom, whole and balanced, liberated, making healthy choices—I'm feeling emotional freedom and doing what I love and loving what I do.

As a psychotherapist, I have seen many clients who have struggled with relationships they don't understand. They, too, have been cheated on and lied to, and they felt feelings of inadequacy, worthlessness, betrayal, and loss.

The purpose of writing this book is to provide the guidance and wisdom to guide you, the reader, along your path to healing if you have been devastated from betrayal. I want to provide compassionate teaching so you can become resilient and live your best life, regardless of your past. I know that for my own soul growth and evolvement, I am here to do this work, and I knew for me to be able to guide others, I had to heal myself first. I am 62 years old, and I can tell you honestly, it's never too late.

I wrote this book to teach and encourage you that no matter what obstacle and challenge you are going through, you can choose to heal. You can choose love over fear and rise to resilience. We all have a wise self that is very much a part of us, perhaps at the subconscious level, that we can awaken and draw on to re-create ourselves. I did.

I feel the desire to share my own story along with my clinical knowledge about betrayal. We are all human, and we are here to learn. As I share my story from my own perspective, I feel it is important for readers to understand that betrayal can happen to anyone, and more significantly, one can rise to resilience. I will share my initial feelings of how something was "off," even though I really didn't understand why, as well as the shame and embarrassment that captured me while ignoring the red flags that were there all along. I used the excuse, "When you're in it, you just don't see it." I will explore the spectrum of empaths and their sensitivities and gifts. I will provide detail about the spectrum of narcissism and cluster B personality disorders and why empaths and narcissists become intimate partners. I will offer protection strategies that empaths can use to protect themselves from narcissists who lack empathy and are not capable of true intimacy, authenticity, harmony, and love. We will explore family of origin as it relates to development, an important component in the selection of intimate partners. It is my wish for you that you learn to spot and cope with extreme narcissism, because that is high on the empath spectrum. These character-disturbed people can leave you living with betrayal and post-traumatic stress disorder, among other types of physical, psychological, and spiritual discord. It is also my wish that you will begin to understand more about yourself, the empath within you, and even the occasional narcissistic behaviors you have and the underlying cause when your defensive reactions are in high gear, especially your defense against your own pain. I call them "energy vampire" days. We all have them, but there is a real difference between having those moments where we can drain others and being a true narcissist. It's no wonder I slept an average of 9 to 10 hours a night when I was married. I was drained and didn't even realize it! If you are in a relationship with an energy vampire, your energy is drained and you are subconsciously trying to figure out a way to replenish yourself.

I will discuss narcissism in the following chapters and the spectrum as well. Narcissists basically present themselves in a good light because they want to win. They have an inflated sense of self-importance, and they have a lack of empathy for others, although they may not show that outwardly. They seek adoration and attention from everyone because they feel so empty, inadequate, and defective at the core level. They fear losing and that they could be exposed for who they truly are—tortured souls. Often, we don't spot them until the betrayal has occurred and it's too late. As in my situation, many narcissists have learned to disguise their shadow traits and exist with a facade self. They wear a mask so they better manipulate people with their charm. Narcissism is a spectrum of psychological illness affecting as much as

5% of the population, more men than women. They hurt us, and they create drama and chaos. What they don't want us to know is how defective they feel while they are so destructive to our psyches. At times they may appear indifferent; however, don't let that fool you, because it matters to them how they are seen. They cannot tolerate criticism or rejection themselves, but they are quick to launch it onto you. They have a way of projecting and blaming you for their own mistakes and shortcomings. The slightest challenge to their fragile self-esteem may trigger a response of narcissistic rage or passive-aggressive behavior, so you feel attacked and they will get satisfaction from hurting you back so they can have the last laugh.

By developing resilience, you will recognize the clarity within yourself, and with that clarity you will have the desire and ability to return to wholeness. When you are whole and balanced, you will attract and manifest what your true desires are.

Narcissism exists in people from all walks of life, not just celebrities or rock stars; a covert narcissist may be occupying the home next door. There are many leaders, CEOs, government officials, lawmakers, medical practitioners, and a multitude of others who take advantage of our lives. In our current culture, it seems as though there are more narcissists than not. I have adolescent clients calling each other narcissists. I realize they are not aware of the actual clinical definition and the complexity of the continuum of narcissism; rather, they heard the term somewhere and decided to use it because it sounds so adult. Last year, a fifteen-year-old female came to me and said, "My dad is a narcissist." I don't know her father; therefore, I cannot say that he is or isn't a narcissist. However, she described his behavior and, from what she described, it would lead one to believe he has narcissistic traits.

Even after we are personally healed from narcissism, it continues to surround us globally, nationally, and locally. We question why we have certain leaders who separate and divide rather than unite. Is narcissism winning, and are we simply accepting it? Have we all been programmed early on that we aren't enough or worthy, not adequate at some level? Is the source the breakdown of the family unit?

Those who continue to believe that we are separate from one another live with false selves and will never really be free to thrive and live from their own true essence. The first step is to turn inward and realize we came here on this planet Earth as bright lights, and we can stand in the light and be loyal to our own true self. That is enough. We are enough. The tools in this book will help you to be able to identify your subconscious programming, deprogram your irrational subconscious beliefs, and free yourself from any blockages of inner trauma. You are reading this book because you have a willingness to heal, and with that, anything is possible. We have been given beautiful gifts to use on our path to healing and emotional freedom.

You will learn to recover your trust and faith in yourself and others after trauma, deception, and betrayal. You will experience love again, but it is important to remember that it always must begin with yourself. You will learn self-love tools throughout these chapters.

As I offer my story and perspective, and as you navigate through your journey, wherever you are in your own progression, see it as a blessing in disguise, as difficult as that may seem. We are here to learn, and there are many lessons for us. Although the journey may seem unjust, unfair, unreasonable, and incredibly painful, and you cannot fathom how your soul could have possibly signed up for this, you can and will come through on the other side more resilient than ever.

"THE INSTINCTS ARE A FAR BETTER PROTECTION THAN ALL THE INTELLECTUAL WISDOM IN THE WORLD."

—CARL JUNG

Chapter One

A Ceremony to Remember

January 2, 2011, I woke up early to find a lovely morning. It was exactly what I expected to manifest: a beautiful day for a wedding, my wedding. I snuck out of my downstairs apartment while my out of town friends were sleeping upstairs. I wanted to have an hour alone with my dogs on the beach before the festivities began. My beach walk with my two yellow labs, Annie and Archie, one and two years old at that time, was pleasant and perfect.

I was calm, yet waves of excitement and anticipation fluttered throughout my body. I was all smiles, believing yet feeling a bit numb about what was about to occur.

I was going to be married in the beautiful quaint chapel on Captiva Island, Florida, at 4:30.

This would be my last morning as a single woman, I thought. It has just been me for so long, 53 years. On my beach walk watching the beautiful sunrise and Ana and Archie playing and swimming over the tiny waves, I knew the day was going to be perfect. And it was. I lived a long happy life without a husband, and now it was my turn to expand my life. Finally, my world was totally complete. I always felt complete, yet yearned for someone to be with to expand my wonderful life. I was present throughout the entire ceremony, beaming. I didn't want to miss one second of the happiest moments of my life. I especially remember "as long as we both shall live." It was so meaningful at the time. I married into a lovely family; two daughters and three adorable grandchildren who were in the wedding.

From the Beginning

"YOUR TASK IS NOT TO SEEK LOVE BUT TO FIND ALL THE BARRIERS WITHIN YOURSELF THAT YOU HAVE BUILT AGAINST LOVE."
—RUMI

My story is truthfully written from my own personal experience and perspective. The names have been changed to protect the guilty.

It's over. I heard these two words in September 2017 through the phone calls, e-mails, and texts from friends who lived in Florida. They were referring to hurricane Irma, which was predicted to be one of the worst hurricanes in history. I replied with those same two words, it's over, only I was referring to my divorce.

Throughout my adulthood, I was in various relationships that tended to be long-term. For some reason or another, my intuition told me that each person was not going to be my forever partner in life. I would go for years not dating and just focusing on my career. Although I had many wonderful friends and a full life, I always had an inkling that someone would show up, perhaps later in life, and that is what happened.

I always wanted to have a life partner to expand my already happy world.

I knew my husband-to-be because he was a practicing chiropractor on the island where I lived in Florida. I had been clinically treated by him on occasion throughout the years.

About seven months after he lost his wife, he seemed to want to get to know me more. I thought it was because he felt comfortable with the fact that he knew me from his practice and knew a little about me. It wasn't long after that he let me know he wanted to spend time with me, and it was obvious he wanted to start a relationship. I felt it was a bit soon after his wife's passing, but my male friends said men have difficulty being alone and they want to move on with someone. We were married one year to the day of our going on an afternoon social date. The more time I spent with him, the more I felt we had in common and we were a good match. It appeared that we both wanted the same things in a partnership, and we had many of the same wishes and dreams. Why not be together? He was almost fifteen years my senior, but he didn't seem like it. He was active and in good shape, and it felt as though we were much closer in age. The age difference didn't affect me at all.

He proposed after only five months of courtship. I was a bit taken aback, but then I thought to myself, why wait? We are older and we both seem to know what we want. He wanted me to have the wedding I never had, so we agreed to around 120 guests. I did like the idea of celebrating with family and friends. For me, it was huge, because at some point before he came into my life, I had accepted the fact that perhaps I would never be married.

After we were married was when I really began to see the true person I had committed to.

There were red flags prior to the marriage, but for the most part, I chose to ignore them. I did call him out on a few of his behaviors, and I would get either the silent treatment, a lie, or a great deal of resistance. As much as I wanted to believe that I knew him, I didn't.

In reflection, there were constant red flags, and I somehow learned to not only ignore, but also navigate my way around them, above them, or below them, just not through them because they kept returning.

If anyone would have said to me when I got married that I would be divorced in six and a half years, I would have told them they were crazy. I doubt if many people at the time of their marriage feel that if it doesn't work out, they can always just get a divorce. People marry because they commit to "till death do us part," and in our vows, "as long as we both shall live." Then life happens. Reality sets in and issues arise. We've all heard the sayings, hindsight is 20/20 and love is blind. I've repeated those words over and over many times since my separation and divorce.

In six and one half years of marriage I learned as much if not more than my graduate and doctoral studies combined! It really is true that we have to experience our own story to really understand the dynamics that play out, no matter how much schooling we have had.

Personal relationship trauma can be devastating. I know subconsciously I signed up for this. Why? It was a part of my life's journey. I believe we come here to Earth school to learn lessons. We either learn them and move on, or we have to repeat them.

I know now that one of the reasons I married the person I did was to heal—heal the unhealed wounded parts of my inner self once and for all. Those parts that unconsciously were attracted to this type of person in the first place. All of my life I gave up pieces of myself for approval of others, to be liked, to have friends, to have boyfriends, and to be married. It's not like I said to myself, "I'm attracted to this man so I can heal the past wounds that I've yet to heal, so I have to put myself through hell and back." No, again, this was totally unconscious. (I use unconscious and subconscious interchangeably.) I even went so far as to celebrate because he was not an alcoholic! (I experienced dating an alcoholic in a previous relationship.) Yippee, I broke the cycle! Unfortunately, however, I only partially broke the cycle by marrying a man who was not an alcoholic,. What I didn't see was that he had the characteristics of a full-blown narcissistic personality disorder.

My betrayal and abandonment all started early in my life when I was only two years old. My biological father and mother divorced, and my father betrayed and abandoned me. This was a toxic mile marker. Of course, I did not consciously realize it at the time, and I grew up without the nuclear family and was shamed because of it in the parochial elementary school I went to because every other child had a mother and father in the household. After much study of psychology and learning about childhood development in my years of schooling, I understood the meaning of abandonment and betrayal on a clinical level, yet I had not processed it within myself and still carried core unhealed wounds and beliefs that I was inadequate. What was it within me that kept attracting the wrong men my whole adult life?

According to psychologist Erik Erikson, the age of two concerns itself developmentally with the stage of shame vs. autonomy. In this second stage of life, one either develops a sense of autonomy and healthy self-esteem due to successful mentoring and parenting or one develops shame as a result of feeling "I am bad, not good enough, wrong, inadequate, unworthy, helpless, unloved, etc." If one becomes stuck in this stage with shame, this feeling remains in the subconscious mind, and one continues feeling this way into adulthood and in relationships.

Every time I was with a partner and that person left me, it was a trigger from the time I was a two-year-old being abandoned. I just had not processed it. My marriage was no different. No, my husband didn't ask for a divorce, yet unacceptable behaviors occurred that would lead any sane wife to have the wherewithal to get out. Thank God I did... in the nick of time.

The Soul Knows What the Conscious Mind Does Not

In my situation, I found out after I married my husband that, in my opinion, he didn't have the ability to commit and remain loyal and faithful. Why? I'll never know for sure, yet I have my suspicions. From my own training, I know that our early wounds give us the chance for repair through relationships later in life. The early trauma of betrayal, abandonment, and feeling unloved not only creates a propensity to revisit similar experiences later in life, but also provides an opportunity to repair these conditions. However, often the early trauma is re-triggered, only for the old wounds to resurge and bring on new hurt and pain. In terms of my husband, my guess is that he may have experienced some form of trauma in his early developmental years that he never addressed. It was repressed, and he built up psychological defenses to protect himself. At his core, however, I believe he was a tortured soul. Although he was married previously, his kind and loving wife became ill and passed away. At the time, I thought that marrying a widower was going to be a positive and happy experience because he knew marriage, and who better could help me through adjusting to my first marriage than a partner who had a long marital history. I later read the research that narcissists can be married for a long time. If you are with a narcissist, and you decide to stay, it is highly likely you will get sick, most often suffering from an autoimmune disease. I have worked with women who lived with or were married to narcissists and also suffered from irritable bowel syndrome (IBS), chronic stress, fibromyalgia, cancer, and various other illnesses and diseases. In my own circumstance, I didn't get sick, yet if I had stayed longer, I know I would have. Finding compassion for someone who so deeply hurts and betrays the partner he is supposed to love takes working through the grief stages and developing an understanding of the potential reasons for the betrayal.

I cannot emphasize enough how very important it is to seek professional help as soon as possible, rather than think you can get through this alone. It's just too damn hard. Although time heals wounds, remember, it's what you do with the time, and seeking out a trained therapist who understands betrayal and narcissism will be your best option.

I want to emphasize that not all narcissists are males. There are female narcissists; however, usually they are more likely to be diagnosed as having borderline personality disorder, which is identified as one of the cluster B personality disorders that I will be referring to in the following chapter.

Red Flags Flying High

The warning signs (red flags, or as I call them, poppies that emerge from the ground) were present all along prior to my marriage—the control, manipulation, put downs, silent treatments, what he didn't say, what he did say, his need for adoration and other women's worshiping. He chose me, not those other women who threw themselves at him. Why should I have any reason to believe that he wouldn't be faithful? However, like many of us do, I chose to ignore those signs because I believed in the expansion of marriage, commitment, loyalty, and partnership, and I trusted him. Call it what you wish. To me, marriage was the ultimate gift in my later years, and after all, I had a career and worked hard all of my life. I was ready for an expansion in my life. It took me 53 years to find who I thought was my Mr. Right! I was older and had life experience with dating, short- and long-term relationships, and live-in relationships, and I was a psychotherapist. Surely this was all a perfect recipe for a happy, healthy marriage.

Intellectually, I knew what it took to make a marriage work. I had counseled thousands of clients on successful coupleship. So why on earth did my marriage not succeed?

I'm a firm believer that it takes two to dance the dance. In reflection, I see clearly what my role was and why attempting to make it right and make the efforts I did were not successful. When my intuition told me that something wasn't quite right prior to the marriage, there were times I used confrontation and times I shut down. Looking back, I realize I needed the balance of just staying calm and having a discussion to see what we could resolve together. I still believe to this day that communication is the key, and I don't believe either one of us fulfilled that need. I did tell him that in order for the marriage to continue after the betrayal we had to go to intensive couples counseling. He made up excuses, and I finally realized he was acting as though he was interested, when in fact, he never had any intention of repairing our marriage.

One major key was that while I always believed that behavior must be in alignment with what a person says, there were many gaps within what I witnessed. As time went on, this seemed to be more of a common theme in the marriage—less communication and more behavior not being in alignment with what was said, at least from my perspective in observing my husband. Turns out, he was not in alignment with what he said as I discovered lie on top of lie. It got to the point that I really didn't know what to believe, yet I still wanted to believe in him, the charming man I thought I married. Turns out that love was a lie, as well.

The entire marriage was filled with a feeling that something was "off," and I found myself walking on eggshells and often being given the silent treatment. What is the silent treatment? It is what narcissists use to inflict punishment and control over their victims. It causes emotional distress, and the victim is often made to feel that she or he has said or done something wrong. This silent treatment is a learned behavior that is established as a coping technique for power and control. Why does one control? Out of fear. When I was in it, I didn't fully understand why this was happening. I would ask myself what I said or did that upset him to the point of ignoring me. The silent treatments would last an average of three days. I would shut down during that time, because I didn't quite know how to handle his mood swings, yet on a deeper level I really didn't think I did anything to push him away. I have learned since these occurrences that there are reasons for this behavior, and no, I wasn't going crazy. I believe my soul knew all along that this marriage was a mistake. He was so dashing and charming in the courtship for the most part, although there were silent treatments used as a form of punishment and control so I would be emotionally stressed and come running to give him supply of attention and adoration. Yes, control and superiority was huge, and as long as he had control, everything was fine. Once those control wheels fell off, he became more insecure and planned his exit strategy, knowing quite well who my replacements would be. Yet, being the type of person I am, I wanted to make every effort—I took him on trips, cooked to my best ability, purchased tickets to events, communicated the best I could, and tried to be cheerful and positive and make things right. It boiled down to "damned if I do and damned if I don't." Nothing seemed to make him happy, and he seemed quite bored with me—so bored that he spent much of his time e-mailing, texting, and talking on the phone with another woman. He even went and stayed in the beachfront condo she arranged for him to stay in when he visited her.

If I was so wrong from the beginning by not being threatened by another woman when I should have been, how on earth could I ever begin to trust myself again? Was I a complete failure? I was duped. It took time for me to trust myself and others. Below are some of the most important things I did with the time that helped me to emerge feeling whole and balanced again:

- I grieved, a necessary part of the healing process. I will discuss this in Chapter 2.
- I sought counseling immediately once I knew my suspicions were confirmed.
- I went through Eye Movement Desensitization and Reprocessing (EMDR) for trauma.
- I did self-hypnosis and guided imagery so I could focus on what I wanted to create for myself.
- I watched my eating behavior because I didn't have much of an appetite, and my dietitian friend was a huge help in reminding me of which healthy foods to focus on.
- I kept exercising. This helped with overcoming the reactionary depression.

- I continued to work because this took the focus off of myself and onto my clients.
- I used self-soothing techniques: I walked and hiked in nature with my dogs, read a lot, got plenty of rest, took Epsom salt baths, soaked in mineral springs, did healing ceremonies, and gave thanks for what I had.
- I meditated daily and became grounded and centered before I left for work.

I had a lot of anger to work through, which I will admit took over a year. Anger is a part of the grief process, and it was a huge part of grief to overcome. It was such a loss of an opportunity I chose to have, that it was as though the dark night of the soul set in. We get through dark journeys, though.

The Conscious and Subconscious Minds

I want to address the conscious and subconscious minds because of their importance throughout our life and the decisions we make. Our conscious mind or "self-consciousness" uses the left side of our logical brain. It has the ability to create plans for the future and think in the past. We analyze, rationalize, and problem solve through our conscious mind. The conscious mind can use its resources to focus on a specific situation, such as getting up and going to work.

Meanwhile, your subconscious mind is on autopilot and lives in the present. According to author Bruce Lipton, our subconscious is quite powerful and operates 95% of the time. I like to use the example of driving. We go from point A to point B, and when we reach our destination, we think, how did I get here? You don't remember that stoplight and turning left, and then driving on Elm Street to get home. If you were not consciously driving from point A to point B, then who was? Your subconscious mind was at the helm! While you did not realize that your subconscious mind was at the helm, it obviously knew what it was doing as you consciously focused on something or someone else. Our subconscious mind takes over when our conscious mind is not paying attention. It includes hidden desires, memories, and drives. It has been programmed by others, especially in our first seven years of life by our parents, teachers, and authority figures who were present in our daily life. We have held onto these subconscious beliefs, and they never went away. If our subconscious mind was programmed with negative messages and we absorbed that information, chances are likely that we continue to have those same programs in our subconscious minds and we can often self-sabotage things our conscious mind wants to succeed with. According to Lipton, the two minds are truly a phenomenal mechanism, yet they can go awry. The conscious mind is the "self," the voice of our own thoughts. It can have great plans for the future filled with love, health, happiness, and prosperity. While we focus on our conscious happy thoughts, who is running the show? Our subconscious. Our subconscious manages our affairs exactly how it was programmed.

For example, say you want to try out for the tennis team. You consciously think you have a chance of making it. Yet, subconsciously, you struggle to feel you are worthy because you had early programming that you messed up and were not good enough at something you attempted to do earlier in life. So you sabotage your efforts in making the team because of negative subconscious programming. Your subconscious mind makes those gut-level intuitive decisions while your conscious mind has to gather and weigh information before decision making.

There were parts of me that subconsciously thought perhaps I wasn't a good enough wife, person, lover, or even professional to be married to this man who so many worshiped. For a period of time I ignored the lies, manipulation, and as mentioned the silent treatments, acts of not caring and projection. Perhaps at some level I didn't feel worthy to be with the "pillar of the community." Why? It was my programming.

The Unconscious Act of Projection

"THERE IS NO SUCH THING AS A PROBLEM WITHOUT A GIFT FOR YOU IN ITS HANDS. YOU SEEK PROBLEMS BECAUSE YOU NEED THEIR GIFTS."
—RICHARD BACH

Projection is an unconscious defense mechanism whereby one projects onto another what is really going on within oneself. This defense mechanism begins early in life. Projection stems from unconscious feelings and unwanted parts of oneself. I found this to be quite common in my marriage with regard to my husband's perceived behaviors. It was apparent to me that he projected onto me what he didn't want to see or admit within himself as a way of diverting his early pain.

I was told on several accounts: "You just want a rich man." "Our marriage is conditional." "You use the word *can't*." "This is not a marriage." Why was he saying these things to me? Why was he angry towards me? Was he overwhelmed, unhappy, dissatisfied with me? Did he feel he made a mistake? Was he threatened by me? What was I doing or saying to make him feel this isn't a marriage? I continued to look into myself and wonder what I could possibly be doing wrong to displease him, a common action one takes thinking they are to blame.

Projection prevents what one doesn't like about the self to look at the other person and think it's all his or her doing, when in fact, it is the projector him or herself. The projector does not want to acknowledge these thoughts, feelings, and behaviors because instinctually, they are fears based on the projector's insecurities about him- or herself. Once I was able to see what was happening clearly, I realized I was made the scapegoat for his insecurities and his blame for whomever hurt him long ago. I doubt he ever processed his pain. What he thought he wanted to complete him began to make sense to me—a rich woman and unconditional love that perhaps he never had nor felt he had—and he had no clue how to achieve this. He thought about what he couldn't do at the core, he was so insecure, and he didn't know how to make the marriage work. After I filed for dissolution of marriage, he told my mother that I had a "psychiatric disorder," and what I do know is that if I would have stayed in the marriage, I may have developed one.

Our Shadow Side

"IF YOU'RE GOING THROUGH HELL, KEEP GOING!"
—WINSTON CHURCHILL

Psychiatrist Carl Jung stated the shadow is the unknown dark side of the personality. According to Jung, the shadow, being instinctive and irrational, is prone to psychological projection in which a perceived personal inferiority is recognized as a perceived moral deficiency in someone else. The shadow is the sum of all personal and collective psychic elements that, because of their incompatibility with the chosen conscious attitude, are denied expression in life. Indeed, Jung differentiated between the personal shadow and the impersonal or archetypal shadow, which acknowledges transpersonal, pure, or radical evil (symbolized by the Devil and demons) and collective evil, exemplified by the horrors of the Nazi holocaust. Literary and historical figures like Adolf Hitler, Charles Manson, and Darth Vader personify the shadow embodied in its most negative, archetypal human form.

Through this entire ordeal, I had to confront my own shadow side and go through my own dark night of the soul in order to emerge whole and healthy. I had to confront myself and ask: How did I get here? Why did I get here? Why did I allow him to push my buttons? What was my own role? What was my defensive style? Was this past life karma? What kind of a wake-up call is this? How can I come to terms and forgive myself for being so blind? Why did I put up with this insidious behavior as long as I did? What was it within me that yet again attracted a narcissist? Could I ever feel compassion again?

Part of me knew and part of me didn't want to know because I had to face my shame and realize I didn't get the lesson I thought I got when I thought I broke the cycle with this person.

My Own Dark Night of the Soul

A long-time reader of Carl G. Jung's work, I learned that what Jung referred to as "The Dark Night of the Soul," is a rite of passage, a traditional time of deep inner struggle and conflict where there is an immersion into the unconscious. What was wrong with my inner guidance system and my inner compass, which guided me to remain on my path?

It was as though I had been dropped into a deep abyss and I felt as though I was dying, physically, emotionally, and spiritually. My faith was questioned, I couldn't sleep and eat, I was off my daily physical routine. I feel that my dogs saved my life or I wouldn't have gotten out of bed! What clearly was going on that I didn't know then and know now was what Jung describes as a "spiritual crisis." Jung referred to any crisis over the age of 30 as being a spiritual crisis. I was over 30 and I was betrayed. Of course, this was a spiritual crisis. It was a time to learn how to return to myself from the depths of betrayal.

Although I was able to sustain living with his behaviors early in the marriage, I became more weary of them as time went on. When we disagreed and he shut down, I too shut down because when I confronted him, we ended up in a vicious cycle and got nowhere.

I learned that if I went to dinner with a girlfriend, I was going to get the silent treatment regardless of offering to bring him dinner and being kind. I gave away pieces of my self and soul to avoid confrontation and silence, and no matter how I attempted to make it better, I would end up disappointed because I felt I couldn't please him if I wasn't with him 24/7. Narcissists tend to isolate their partners because they don't want them to have friends or be successful. If I was working for him, that was fine because I was within his sight and I was under his control. Once I decided to build my own private counseling practice in Colorado, he was greatly threatened. I was reprimanded if I didn't work much, and I was reprimanded if I worked all day and wasn't home with him.

Finally, there came a time when I realized I was a third wheel. He had someone else, emotionally that is. It didn't take a therapist to figure out what was going on with the phone calls, texts, and e-mails. He began taking trips back to Florida to "work," yet I knew he was spending time with her. I even found out that he was seeing other women as well. No wonder I felt an inner resentment toward him. A part of me knew before I consciously put it all together and received confirmation of this.

Upon confronting him, he denied my accusations, lied to me, threw it all back in my face, and attempted to make me feel like the guilty one. It didn't work. As traumatized as I was, a deep part of me knew that if I was not going to become sick, I had to get out of the marriage. After a few months of separation, more lies, and his continuing his affair, I continued to gather evidence, then I filed for divorce. At the time this was happening and prior to filing for divorce, I didn't make the connection that I had post-traumatic stress symptoms (Chapter 2) and I needed to get the help of a professional. When separated, I sought the guidance of an experienced counselor. It was extremely helpful, and I had full support from him. I had the support of my family and friends, and I had what I later called "my team." Many of my team had observed his treatment of me and later told me they saw it all. I also continued to collect evidence such as photos and texts. I knew there was no way there could ever be a reconciliation, especially after I concluded that I was married to someone with a full-blown covert narcissistic personality disorder.

Due to his erratic e-mails and texts, I felt it was in my highest good to go "no contact" with him. This was so helpful in many ways, which will be explained in the next chapter. It was difficult enough not to obsess about him, and I wondered how I could ever get through this and become resilient. I can tell you now, although it varies for everyone, I reiterate that time heals, and it's what you do with the time that helps the most.

I see now that my own dark night of the soul was my rite of passage into a new way of life—a better life, a more sacred life, and such an appreciation for life. I remember my eastern vedic astrologer telling me, "You had to go through it." I didn't understand it at the time. Why? I thought. Didn't I deserve love and happiness with the man I thought I was going to spend the rest of my life with? It just didn't make sense. Now it does. It would have been a lifetime of the same old ways of being treated poorly. I would have remained in a state of "I'm not worthy of real authentic love, there must be something wrong with me." Rather, now I see it as a positive transformation into greater insight and wisdom.

Is there a greater love for me out there? I don't know. What I do know is that although I would love to experience a full spectrum of real authentic love with a life partner, I am open to the invitation.

Time Is on My Side

From my own experience I can tell you that healing takes at least two years, and it can take longer. It is very individualized.

There is no right time to heal. Healing occurs throughout the grief process. Please be patient with yourself, and understand you may not just be healing from a broken relationship or divorce; this trauma could have started early in your life with abandonment, abuse, betrayal, or all of these, and you will have to deprogram this subconscious wounding and reprogram that you are worthy of love, honor, and respect. So much help is available with resources all around the world. No matter where you live, you can get the help you seek so healing, growth, and love of self and life can occur.

Chapter Two

The Trauma of Betrayal

"Very little grows on jagged rock. Be grateful, be crumbled, so wildflowers come up where you are. You've been stony for too many years. Try something different. Surrender."
—Rumi

Trauma changes the brain. According to world-renowned trauma expert and *New York Times* bestselling author Dr. Bessel van der Kolk, once you've been traumatized, you live in a different world. You see the world differently, and you experience yourself differently. You're a changed person. Trauma shatters all of our defenses and leaves us powerless to our most primitive survival strategies.

The symptoms of betrayal parallel those of post-traumatic stress disorder (PTSD). In the mental health field, we know how trauma manifests itself. Studies have consistently shown that structural changes in the brain do occur with PTSD. What this means is that you do not focus and concentrate; you are hypervigilant and anxious, and you find yourself obsessing about the partner who betrayed you.

Studies have shown that 43% of spouses who suffer from betrayal can feel the effects for over two years. I know this from my own experience of betrayal and the experiences of counseling clients who have felt the depths of betrayal. Betrayal is a deliberate act of disloyalty. It is the most raw breach of trust at its core that I can think of. It makes you feel like you are losing your mind. The bewilderment, confusion, anger, depression, and bargaining put you on an emotional roller coaster and pull you in opposite directions until you are feeling so pulled apart and devalued that you find yourself not knowing in which direction to turn.

Those of us who have experienced betrayal know that the more we love and trust, the more we open our hearts and allow another to come into our lives, the deeper the wounds left by betrayal. It affects us on all levels—mind, body, emotional, and spiritual.

I wish that when I was going through the many layers of betrayal in my marriage, I knew then what I know today. More information would have helped me feel normal, and I would have been able to be kinder to myself when my emotions and behavior felt out of control. At the time I did not understand the science and theory behind the way that we pair-bond and what happens when that attachment is damaged. I only knew that discovering sexual betrayal in my relationship was a horrible trigger and resurgence that unconsciously went back to the womb.

It wasn't until my adulthood that my mother shared with me that her husband, my biological father, was having an affair when she was pregnant with me. He told her he couldn't decide who he should choose. My mother chose for herself. She finally left him when I was two years old and took me back to the town where she was born, about two hours from Washington, D.C. This was in 1959, a time when this was essentially unheard of. People didn't divorce, especially those who were Catholic. It was unacceptable. I honor and respect my mother for having the where-with-all to leave. How very frightening that must have been. She moved us into her mother's home, where my grandmother and great uncle raised me while she, as a single mother, worked. Although this was so rare in those days, I did have a friend up the street whose mother was divorced as well. I was not alone, at least outside of the classroom.

I attended a Catholic school from first through part of sixth grade. I was an outcast because my parents were divorced. I was asked why I didn't live with both my mother and father. The nuns didn't accept me; rather, they were verbally abusive, and if I tried to get close to them at recess, they literally pushed me away. I am aware of the magnitude of people who were shamed, humiliated, and physically, sexually, and emotionally abused by the nuns and priests, and it's truly horrifying how betrayal existed in the Catholic schools.

We went to school believing that our teachers, including the priests and nuns, would be the adults away from home that we could trust. Yet that trust often was breached, replaced by the horrifying brutality that took place against innocent young children. Is it any wonder that countless adults are coming out and filing claims against the Catholic diocese for crimes committed against them?

My trust was breached three times in childhood. First, by my biological father; second, by the priests, nuns, and lay teachers at the Catholic school; and third, by a man who was a Girl Scout leader who fondled me and made me promise not to tell anyone. I blocked it for many years, as so many children of abuse do. Fortunately for me, the man treaded lightly, and I don't think it lasted long from my faint memory.

When someone goes through the rawness of betrayal, they experience a gut-wrenching breach in trust that changes life as they know it, and it can be embedded in one's psyche forever. It's such an emotional blow realizing that your partner has manipulated, lied, and kept secrets to hide their insidious behaviors. What may have started in childhood with a breach of trust is repeated in adulthood when that very trust is breached again. As if going through earthquakes in childhood wasn't enough, the intensity and magnitude of another in adulthood does rock your world and is even higher on the Richter scale and additional poison to one's soul.

For me, it was largely the embarrassment of suspecting my husband was having at the very least an emotional affair, yet not really doing anything about my suspicions until I heard from others that this was indeed going on. Upon reflection, I suppose a part of me was in denial, our chief defense that protects us from pain. I didn't want to think about it.

I chose to believe him, that he was her "spiritual counselor." I just went with it, never thinking it could or would cross over into a full-blown affair.

Betrayal can be a complete shock and surprise to the system. The long-term effects impact how one can trust again, feel a sense of safeness, and learn that it's okay to be vulnerable as one re-enters the world of uncertainty.

When I confronted my husband for the second time and blatantly accused him of having an affair, I was in an altered state of mind. I had just received a phone call with confirmation that his affair had been going on for two years. It was as though a part of me emerged that I never knew existed. I was highly charged with fear and rage as the flood gates opened. Of course, according to him, the betrayer, I was the crazy one and had a "psychiatric disorder," and he was tired of the "drama." Drama? And just who created the drama? What control and manipulation. His accusations threw me into a tailspin of trauma, which was my drama.

What is trauma? According to trauma expert Dr. Bessel Van der Kolk, trauma is "An emotional wound or shock that creates substantial lasting damage to the psychological development of the person."

For many people, including myself, it was not so much the affair that caused so much pain; rather, it was the dishonesty and breach of trust. The belief in the spouse is shattered, and this betrayal of trust is particularly traumatic.

Psychologists, counselors, and psychiatrists refer to a diagnostic manual (*Diagnostic and Statistical Manual of Mental Disorders*, DSM-5) to determine the criteria of certain psychological disorders. The following are the criteria for PTSD:

DSM-5 Criteria for PTSD

(1). All of the criteria are required for the diagnosis of PTSD. The following text summarizes the diagnostic criteria:

Criterion A (one required): The person was exposed to: death, threatened death, actual or threatened serious injury, or actual or threatened sexual violence, in the following way(s):

- Direct exposure
- Witnessing the trauma
- Learning that a relative or close friend was exposed to a trauma
- Indirect exposure to aversive details of the trauma, usually in the course of professional duties (e.g., first responders, medics)

Criterion B (one required): The traumatic event is persistently re-experienced, in the following way(s):

- Intrusive thoughts

- Nightmares
- Flashbacks
- Emotional distress after exposure to traumatic reminders
- Physical reactivity after exposure to traumatic reminders

Criterion C (one required): Avoidance of trauma-related stimuli after the trauma, in the following way(s):

- Trauma-related thoughts or feelings
- Trauma-related reminders

Criterion D (two required): Negative thoughts or feelings that began or worsened after the trauma, in the following way(s):

- Inability to recall key features of the trauma
- Overly negative thoughts and assumptions about oneself or the world
- Exaggerated blame of self or others for causing the trauma
- Negative affect
- Decreased interest in activities
- Feeling isolated
- Difficulty experiencing positive affect

Criterion E (two required): Trauma-related arousal and reactivity that began or worsened after the trauma, in the following way(s):

- Irritability or aggression
- Risky or destructive behavior
- Hypervigilance
- Heightened startle reaction
- Difficulty concentrating
- Difficulty sleeping

Criterion F (required): Symptoms last for more than 1 month.

Criterion G (required): Symptoms create distress or functional impairment (e.g., social, occupational).

Criterion H (required): Symptoms are not due to medication, substance use, or other illness.

Two specifications:

- Dissociative Specification. In addition to meeting criteria for diagnosis, an individual experiences high levels of either of the following in reaction to trauma-related stimuli:
  - Depersonalization. Experience of being an outside observer of or detached from oneself (e.g., feeling as if "this is not happening to me" or one were in a dream).
  - Derealization. Experience of unreality, distance, or distortion (e.g., "things are not real").
- Delayed Specification. Full diagnostic criteria are not met until at least six months after the trauma(s), although onset of symptoms may occur immediately.

Note: DSM-5 introduced a preschool subtype of PTSD for children ages six years and younger.

Today, therapists are beginning to acquire insight into the traumatic, long-term emotional effects of betrayal by a close partner. Therapists who are working with clients who experience marital infidelity and relationship betrayal have become much more open to spotting and treating the often fragile, rollercoaster emotional states of spouses who have been cheated on and betrayed.

Trauma caused by spousal betrayal typically manifests in the following ways:

- *Emotional lability:* Feeling excessive emotional feelings, reactions, and behaviors, including mood shifts, crying jags, and emotions ranging from sadness to anger and rage.
- *Symptoms of PTSD:* Grief stages (discussed later in this chapter); sleeplessness, nightmares, hypervigilance, anxiety, rage, fear, difficulty focusing on day-to-day living.
- *Obsessive thoughts:* Frequent distractions of the trauma, complicated grief, struggle to focus on day-to-day activities.
- *Isolation:* Staying alone for prolonged periods of days, weeks, even months.
- *Compulsive behaviors:* For example, excessive spending, eating, exercising, gambling, or promiscuity.
- *Avoidance:* Will not think about or discuss the trauma. Avoidance is the number one coping technique.
- *Self-protective behaviors:* These include constantly checking phone messages, texts, e-mails, and Facebook.

Betrayal/Trauma Bonding

"TRAUMATIZED PEOPLE CHRONICALLY FEEL UNSAFE INSIDE THEIR BODIES: THE PAST IS ALIVE IN THE FORM OF GNAWING INTERIOR DISCOMFORT. THEIR BODIES ARE CONSTANTLY BOMBARDED BY VISCERAL WARNING SIGNS, AND, IN AN ATTEMPT CONTROL THESE PROCESSES, THEY OFTEN BECOME EXPERT AT IGNORING THEIR GUT FEELINGS AND IN NUMBING AWARENESS OF WHAT IS PLAYED OUT INSIDE. THEY LEARN TO HIDE FROM THEIR SELVES."

—BESSEL VAN DER KOLK, *THE BODY KEEPS THE SCORE*

Most likely you have shared with your narcissist partner a trauma bond. This type of bond, although toxic, is a very powerful dynamic because of the chemical cascade of hormones that is involved and released. This rollercoaster relationship, which you most likely will relate to and perhaps even crave, is often due to the environmental pattern of the life your narcissist was raised in. This may have occurred as a result of neglect and feelings of emptiness the narcissist experienced growing up. Narcissists thrive on all of the drama and chaos because that is the known and familiar, which has nothing to do with you, yet you take it on. If you were raised in this way, you may be susceptible to this same drama and chaos as well. Put this dynamic together, and you have a toxic enmeshment. Only thing is, the narcissist won't take ownership of this type of family dynamic and will project it all onto you. It can recapitulate what happened in your own childhood, and the feeling of abandonment is re-created again, leaving you powerless and full of fear. We do things out of fear that are not in our highest good, and thus, we have a vicious addictive cycle of pain. Your feelings do not matter to the narcissist, regardless of what they are. The *only* thing that matters to the narcissist is that they are getting their supply of whatever it takes from others in order for them to survive. They are incapable of healing, just as they won't ever acknowledge their responsibility. However, *you* are capable of healing—and you will, once you develop the full awareness of why you put up with the abuse, no matter how subtle, and why you were addicted to the chaotic cycle of narcissistic abuse in the first place so you will never allow this to happen again.

I cannot emphasize enough that when one goes though betrayal, it is very difficult to break the connection. This is the biochemical bonding that will be discussed in this chapter. When a partner betrays you, he or she will be cold and aloof, and will devalue and discard you. Then, something called intermittent reinforcement will occur, where the betrayer shifts to a nicer, calmer demeanor to entice you back into the relationship. You are still in a state of shock and reeling from the betrayal. You are biochemically bonded, and all you want to do is reconnect. The paradox is that the mammalian brain is looking for your betraying partner to return and relieve the pain that he or she inflicted on you to begin with! Sadly, you have become intensely focused, obsessed, and fixated beyond any rational state of mind, and you will do anything to reunite with this person. You may loathe this person, and yet at the same time you still love this person. This is referred to as cognitive dissonance. It's a feeling of powerlessness and helplessness, and you succumb to the drama that is continuing. You have heard of the abused child who still loves the parent who is doing the abusing. The child wouldn't think of being without the parent regardless of the emotional, physical, or sexual abuse they're experiencing. It's the same phenomenon experienced by battered spouses. They return to their spouses knowing it can cost them their life. When experiencing trauma bonding, there is no self-regulation, and your nervous system is in a state of shock.

If you have yet to seek professional help, now is the time. It's never too late. Even the reassurance of a trusted friend is important at this time in addition to you receiving professional help. Please know this is a process. This trauma bonding may have started early in your life, and you have just entered the second act of the performance of a betrayer acting out his or her own torturous scene in the play.

As I did in the beginning of this book, it is common to piece together and trace the many aspects of the relationship and discover the missing pieces of the betrayal from when it first began. I know for myself, my sleep pattern had not been the same since that fateful day of confirming what my intuition had been telling me for years. As I experienced several of the above manifestations, I see now it was all a part of the trauma of being betrayed. After two years, my eating behavior is just starting to normalize. My weight loss stemmed from not eating much for a year, yet I ate healthy foods because I knew food was my fuel and healthy nutrition was essential.

Although I knew at times I just wanted to be alone and not have to obsess about it, I had no one. He had women all over the place, being the womanizer he was. I had a broken heart; his heart was hardened, and he didn't care. I tried to keep up with a regular exercise routine. I volunteered, I read, I wrote, I made a vision board, I moved, I had amazing support, I had counseling, and I had my dogs, thank God. It takes time to heal from this kind of betrayal. I kept hearing that, and I knew that intellectually, but now from experience I know it's true. I thrive, for the most part, and love my life. I know my trauma, like everyone else's, does have an effect on the brain, and we do heal.

Trauma and Its Effects on the Brain

As mentioned at the beginning of this chapter, Bessel van der Kolk, M.D., is a leading authority on trauma. According to van der Kolk, the changes in the brain produced by trauma explain why those who are traumatized by abuse experience a form of hypervigilance as well as paralysis, which Maeir and Seligman refer to as "learned helplessness." Abuse from trauma has repercussions, including the toxic shame, self-blame, and self-loathing survivors feel. Trauma can live in our bodies and minds for many years, sometimes an entire lifetime. Trauma reactions are individualized, but each reaction is valid based on the trauma situation and its impact on the individual. In his book, *The Body Keeps the Score,* van der Kolk states, "We know now that their behaviors are not the result of moral failings or signs of lack of willpower or bad character—they are caused by actual changes in the brain." The same brain circuitry activated when we experience physical pain can be activated when we suffer emotional pain and heartbreak. Heartbreak causes a surge of adrenaline, causing us to respond to an emotional threat as though it were a physical threat. The symptoms include increased heart rate, breathing, blood pressure, and stress hormones, such as a rise in cortisol levels. The brain cannot differentiate between touching a hot stove and betrayal. In both cases, the burn is torturous, and the entire psyche is affected.

Physiologically, in the moment of trauma, the emotional brain signals the release of a cascade of hormones including adrenaline, and the body goes into fight, flight, or freeze mode. Simultaneously, our mammalian brain is discombobulated and cannot sustain normal functioning; hence, we are hypervigilant, and our entire balance and wholeness is out of whack. It's even common for PTSD symptoms to manifest right away or in later months. There are betrayal victims who repress their abandonment and deny their pain for years. They go about their business as if nothing happened; however, the manifestation usually occurs physically with some form of illness, as in an autoimmune disease or cancer.

Brain studies have consistently shown that structural changes occur in the brain from PTSD. The specific regions affected are the amygdala (fear/emotional center), the medial frontal cortex, and the hippocampus (memory center). It becomes difficult to eliminate distressing thoughts, feelings, and memories, leading to obsessive thoughts and hypervigilance, which is all connected to the trauma from betrayal.

When a child is raised by a narcissistic, abusive parent or caretaker, the structure of their brain can be altered and rewired, thus the increase in depression, anxiety, and in some cases suicidal ideation when these children reach adulthood. Specific areas of the brain that are affected by trauma include the frontal cortex (planning cognitive center of the brain), hippocampus (memory center), corpus callosum (helps integrate the two halves of the brain), and amygdala (fear/emotional center). These are some of the same areas affected by PTSD. A victim's reaction to a trauma is through the limbic system (emotional center), which is the reptilian part of the brain where emotions are stored and processed. Hypervigilance, one criteria of PTSD, is due to the resemblance of something to an already experienced trauma. Before I blocked my husband, I would receive erratic texts; the ones that were abusive would re-create the feelings I had of the actual scene when I confronted him and he denied and lied about the affair. I still have flashbacks to something emotionally hurtful that my husband said, and I have a somatic experience. I get a "pit" in my solar plexus that I had for months before I actually confronted him. Sometimes I wake up at night with the same feelings, especially if I had a disturbing dream about him and/or his women. I clearly wanted validation that he was having an affair after he denied it, so I asked for it to come to me in a dream. After a couple of weeks, the dream came. It was crystal clear that they were together. As painful as it was, at least I knew.

Hormones and Their Effect with Trauma

Oxytocin

Oxytocin is known as the "love hormone." When we fall in love, oxytocin is released and promotes a sense of trust with the partner and feelings of love and attachment. It is also known as the "cuddle" hormone, because when we are touched or having sexual interaction, this hormone is also released. When we are abandoned and betrayed, our oxytocin levels are drained away from us. It's a chemical withdrawal, just as if we were withdrawing from an addictive drug. We are hard-wired to live harmoniously and lovingly, so when our oxytocin is removed from us, our nervous system sends out desperate signals to reconnect. This is yet another reason it is so difficult to leave the betrayer, as painful as the hurt is.

Our bond to a partner remains strong as a result of the release of this hormone. Regardless of the partner's abuse and betrayal, we can still release oxytocin through reinforcement of the partner's idealization (i.e., gifts, flowers, compliments, or sex to name a few). The client is rewarded for desired behavior occasionally instead of every time. Sexual relations with the partner also strengthen the toxic bond. This tactic of intermittent reinforcement is simply the partner's tool for keeping the vicious cycle of relationship under his or her control. This behavior often can trigger flashbacks and trauma related to the victim's childhood experiences of abuse/positive reinforcement. What also happens is the abuser conditions the victim so he or she receives less over time from the abuser. In my own scenario, I clearly remember feeling as though I wasn't pleasing my partner, so I upped the ante to get affection. This included taking him on trips; buying tickets to shows, plays, and concerts; and paying for everything. He became conditioned to my efforts at making the relationship good. What did he do? Very little because he knew that if I wanted to attend a show or event or travel, I would take care of it. At times I remember thinking to myself, damned if I do and damned if I don't. Sometimes I felt that nothing was good enough, a recurrent theme that I felt in my childhood with my parents.

Completely severing any contact whatsoever is the healthiest way to heal. This is very difficult, however, because of the intermittent reinforcement (they throw you crumbs) and cognitive dissonance (two different cognitions in the brain; I love him/her, I loathe him/her).

"THE FURTHER WITHIN MYSELF I GO, THE FARTHER OUT INTO THE WORLD I CAN REACH."
—CHAIWAT THIRAPANTU

Cortisol

Abusive, unhealthy relationships go through more highs and lows than a typical, naturally healthy relationship. All relationships have peaks and valleys; however, in an abusive relationship they are more frequent, and subsequently there is an increase in the biochemical bond. For example, cortisol, a stress hormone, gets released during the highs and lows of a toxic relationship. It is released by the adrenal glands in response to fear as a part of "fight or flight." Stress remains in our bodies, and increased levels of cortisol strengthen memories associated with fear. When we have a flashback (a symptom of PTSD), our cortisol levels rise, and fear-based occurrences embed the memories deeper into the neural networks of our brains, making the traumatic memories more intense, and hence more difficult to recover from. Although cortisol drums up fear-based memories, there are some tools you can use to counteract this stress hormone:

- Exercise
- Mindfulness meditation
- Music therapy
- Becoming involved in more social situations
- Learning to laugh, which loosens up the solar plexus

Adrenaline and Norepinephrine

These two stress hormones prepare our body for the fight or flight response. When we are in contact with the person we love, adrenaline is released. When this occurs, we experience a racing heart and sweaty palms. This hormone is also tied to fear. When an intense encounter is experienced with our partner, we are more prone to being drawn to them because fear releases dopamine. This is released in the reward center in our brain, which leads to trauma bonding. It makes sense that couples who have been in the emotional ups and downs of a roller coaster together become more bonded, because the fear establishes a greater biochemical bond. This is why having no contact with a partner during a breakup is so difficult. It's an addiction, if you will, to the pain, emotional trauma, and fear that remains in the vicious cycle of abuse.

Epinephrine increases your heart rate and enables you to move quickly; the hormone norepinephrine is released by the adrenals and causes sympathetic nerves to send blood flow to the large muscle groups and lungs.

Serotonin

This hormone regulates mood; the higher our serotonin levels are, the better we feel. Those with low levels of serotonin are more prone to engage in sexual behavior, which releases oxytocin and dopamine (pleasure center), thus helping to bond the victim and abuser. These hormones interact with each other and no doubt are components that contribute to this cycle. It's no surprise that victims become obsessed with their partners through the fear/love cycle due to these chemical releases.

Sins of Betrayal

When the person you trust eludes the truth after having promised to honestly share their thoughts and feelings with you, it is soul shattering. Two very different worlds collide: theirs, in which they are aware of their opinions, judgments, and struggles concerning you and the relationship; and yours, in which you are not. We experience betrayal and deception when promises, overtly spoken or implied by actions, have been broken without our knowing a decision was being considered. Professing devotion and love while carrying on with someone else or setting it up to exit the relationship are just two examples.

The word *betrayal* comes from the Middle English word *bitrayen*, meaning "mislead, deceive." Being lied to chips away at your soul. Although this kind of betrayal is not always about infidelity, though it often is, it involves deceit, manipulation, exploitation, lies, and the slow undermining and erosion of your self-confidence and identity. In this way, what looks like an everyday breakup or divorce from the outside can hide months or years of half-truths and withholding. The moment when you finally discover the truth of this betrayal, shock, denial, and immense hurt and pain set in. This betrayal reaches the very depths of your soul and can last for years. One thing is for sure: you will never be the same. From this moment on, extreme self-care is needed, including professional counseling to recover yourself. Whatever you do, reach out to find your way to the deep spiritual healing waiting in the depths of your betrayed heart.

Betrayal in Relationship

Betrayal is probably the most devastating loss a person can experience. Betrayal involves someone in the act of violating your trust in them.

Betrayal is when a child is abused and/or neglected by a parent who is supposed to love and protect the child. Betrayal is when someone you trust lies to you, cheats on you, abuses you, or hurts you, putting their self-interest/absorption first. The reason that betrayal is such a huge loss is because it is an act that doesn't have to occur as opposed to loss through a death. It occurs only because of someone's deliberately hurtful behavior, carelessness, or their own personal weakness. The person who was betrayed believes the choice was wrong and very preventable.

If a child was traumatized, the wound carries over into each developmental stage until the trauma is dealt with. If it is not handled, the individual is at high risk for either being retraumatized or traumatizing someone else.

Although we hear the term *infidelity* in our society as the ultimate betrayal, and it is true, there are subtle betrayals that occur in relationships that can lead to the demise of the relationship. Partnership needs to be inclusive of choosing each other day after day and making each other a top priority. If this does not occur, the chance of keeping trust and commitment fades away. Mutual trust, honor, and respect are the major keys in keeping a relationship solid. Anything that violates a committed relationship's contract of mutual trust and respect can end in disaster.

When disloyalty enters the relationship, betrayals are founded on two building blocks:

1. *Deception* (not revealing your true needs to avoid conflict) and a yearning for an emotional connection outside of the relationship
2. *Emotional cheating:* Although some don't believe this behavior exists, it does, and it's a loaded gun ready to shoot down a relationship. Different kinds of relationships develop, whether at work,

the gym, or the coffee shop; e-mailing; texting; or other forms of communication—all spell a threat to the relationship at home. These relationships turn into both people sharing intimate details of their lives. What makes this a slippery slope is if the partner would be uncomfortable knowing this or seeing this behavior and interaction. These non-physical encounters Are just as much of a betrayal as physical ones. They can feel isolating, humiliating, Confusing and hurtful. When a partner's energy is going to another person, the friendship crosses the line and threatens the primary relationship. Here are the signs that your partner's so called "friendship" has crossed the line:

- The friendship is kept hidden and secretive.
- If you question the friendship as a concern of yours, you are dismissed and discarded.
- If you have asked your partner to end the friendship because it has crossed a boundary, and you are told no or lied to that it ended.
- When the boundaries you set have been disrespected.
- This friend is the subject of fantasies during troubled times in the relationship.

If any of these are accurate, then the friendship is too intimate and needs to cease for your partnership to survive.

3. *Physical Infidelity*

- The person shifts emotional attention into a physical/sexual contact.
- Having sexual relations with someone outside of a committed relationship. Unless a couple has an open marriage or commitment, then physical infidelity occurs.

There is no coupleship support when one partner keeps one foot out of the relationship, especially when there is no accountability or ownership of the betrayal. When this occurs, it's not uncommon for the betrayed partner to blame a trigger as the real problem, when it's really the lack of commitment.

A committed relationship requires both partners to be there for each other through simple day-to-day living of life traumas or illnesses. It takes both partners to commit to betrayal-proofing the relationship. One cannot do it for two. When one partner has emotionally and/or physically tuned into someone else, it becomes a huge challenge for the relationship to sustain a coupleship. Both individuals have to want the partnership to last.

"EVERY ACT, THOUGHT AND CHOICE ADDS UP TO THE PERMANENT MOSAIC: OUR DECISIONS RIPPLE THROUGH THE UNIVERSE OF CONSCIOUSNESS TO AFFECT THE LIVES OF ALL. EVERY ACT OR DECISION MADE THAT SUPPORTS LIFE, SUPPORTS ALL LIFE, INCLUDING OUR OWN."

—DAVID R. HAWKINS, M.D., PH.D.

Betrayal and the Grief Process

With betrayal as a loss, it is important and necessary to understand the grief process in order to cope effectively. When people experience betrayal, they have overwhelming emotions that are so intense they are unable to make any sense of them. If you have experienced betrayal, it's imperative that you have an understanding of what these emotions are and why they are coming up for you before you try to come up with an action plan to handle your grief.

There is no right or wrong way to grieve, but it's necessary to go through the grieving process in order to heal. Grief involves stages that will overlap and weave in and out of your life. The grief stages are as follows:

1. *Denial:* Shock. The disbelief that this is actually happening. It's a numb feeling, and no matter how much we know something intuitively, we can never quite prepare for the actual reality of the situation. Denial is our chief protection from pain. We wonder how we can go on, if we can go on, why we should go on. Because grief is so intense, many will avoid the experience of grief because the emotions are so powerful. They tend to engage in avoidance behaviors, the number one coping technique. An avoidance behavior can be an addictive behavior such as using drugs or alcohol, smoking, overeating, or gambling. Sometimes when one loses a relationship, he or she will reach out very quickly for another person to replace the loss of the partner. This is like taking a drug; it's only a temporary solution with no real authentic joy. It's an obsessive reassurance-seeking dependency due to the inability to heal alone. These relationships never last. We try to find a way to simply get through each day. Denial and shock help us to cope and make survival possible. Denial helps us to pace our feelings of grief. There is a grace in denial. It is nature's way of letting in only as much as we can handle. As you accept the reality of the loss and start to ask yourself questions, you are unknowingly beginning the healing process. You are becoming stronger, and the denial is beginning to fade. As you continue with this process, all the feelings you were denying begin to surface.

   I believe my denial started when we were initially dating. As I observed, women threw themselves at him right in front of me. I was not threatened, because he was dating me and they all knew it. We were an item, so why on earth would I have to be threatened by any of these women?

What I came to realize was that he threw out a vibe to them that he was the all-loving guru and it was ok because he loved the adoration. However, the one woman with whom he was entangled all along was the one he talked about "having such a hard time" when we got engaged. That was a red flag. It was always in the back of my mind, and now I see that I was in denial of just how close they really were. I wonder just how many women he had in between his wife's passing and me. I remember thinking it was too soon for us to date because he had lost his wife only seven months prior. For some reason, I thought someone who lost a spouse who was married as long as he was would need at least a year, although I know that grief is a very individual process. My denial continued throughout the courtship and the marriage. He and his "friend" never stopped talking, texting, and e-mailing the entire time we were together. It made me question if the two of them were involved when he was married and kept it secret like they did with me.

2. *Anger:* Anger is a mask for pain. It is very natural to feel anger after betrayal. It's an important emotion to work through because eventually the anger only hurts you. Anger is a necessary stage of the healing process. It is common at this stage for people to become so focused on the wrong done to them that they don't fully understand the overwhelming sadness underneath, which is where the real pain is. Anger is a natural human emotion and needs to be addressed as a part of the grief stages. A person's initial reaction is

to retaliate because they are so upset at the person who hurt them, the betrayer. During this time of anger, it's healthy for the person who is hurting to vent emotions. This can come through talking it out with a friend, counselor, or clergy; writing about it also can be very cathartic. Vent to those who will listen and understand to the best of their ability what you are going through. Hopefully they can validate your anger without feeding your anger.

Be willing to feel your righteous anger, even though it may seem endless. The more you truly feel it, the more it will begin to dissipate and the more you will heal. There are many other emotions under the anger, and you will get to them in time, but anger is the emotion we are most used to managing. The truth is that anger has no limits. A connection made from the strength of anger feels better than nothing. We usually know more about suppressing anger than feeling it. The anger is just another indication of the intensity of your love.

My anger within the marriage began when I had confirmation from other sources that his affair had been going on for two years. "How could he," I thought. Yes, I reacted. And yes, it's automatic to go into an altered state of consciousness when you are hit with such devastating news. The people who shared this devastating news with me were long-time trusted sources. I had known these people for years. I knew they would not lead me astray. I knew they saw the two of them together (which was later confirmed), and when I went on my own search for evidence, it didn't take long to find it with the latest technological advances. My anger was a cover for my hurt and pain. I had been betrayed the entire marriage, the marriage I longed for and hoped would happen someday. I couldn't eat, sleep, or function. I was an absolute mess. I wept, yelled, and cursed him and her as well. Have people's values and morals gone out the window? How could anyone, much less my husband, do such a thing? I simply could not wrap my brain around it, because this is what you watch on TV, read in the tabloids, and I have heard it more than once in my office with clients.

As you work through the anger, you will start to feel a sadness or depression as you come to a realization about the loss. You know there is shattered trust, and you can never get it back. Once someone has violated your trust, you forever know the chance of being betrayed again is there. It can help to write down how you feel—you can imagine telling the betrayer the hurt and pain you have experienced and the loss of the relationship that grieves you. Give yourself permission to cry. Grieving is healing. It is a natural part of the healing that takes place from the different grief experiences we will have in our life. If we can learn to trust the process fully, we will heal. Allow these feelings to be what they are, whatever that means. Feelings are never wrong or bad. Allow the space for them. To feel is to heal. When you begin to trust this process, you will get to a place of acceptance. You will then begin to make decisions that will require action that is in your highest good. You will make the proper decision based on your growth and learning. You may decide that a continued relationship with this person will only lead to more hurt and betrayal and is not worth your effort in trying to sustain a relationship. Or you may decide there are too many positives about the relationship to give up. Listen to your intuition, because intuition always knows.

As grief came and went, weaving in and out, I remember one day feeling like I had this under control, and then the next moment feeling like I was out of control. I never knew what each day would bring. I did know I had to ride the wave, and when the anger came through me that I needed to get it out. Although everyone is different, physical exercise was helpful. Living in the mountains, I found hiking to be so rewarding because I could not only release my anger through each step up the mountain, I was in spirit, inspired by nature. That was my solace. I could also throw rocks down the mountain, and by the time I finished the hike I always felt invigorated and renewed knowing I could make it to the next day. The best healing for me was to let out my anger rather than repress it. We have to face it—anger is a part of grief and has to be dealt with. Repressing it will only lead to depression, and any mismanaged anger style will only linger until you learn healthy coping techniques to manage your anger.

3. *Bargaining:* Bargaining consists of "what ifs" and "if onlys." We get caught up in the woulda, coulda, shouldas. What if I just could have seen it coming? What if I was smarter, wiser, more in-tune, listened to my intuition, and so on? The "if onlys" cause us to find fault in ourselves and what we think we could have done differently. We may even bargain with the pain. We will do anything not to feel the pain of this loss. We remain in the past, trying to negotiate our way out of the hurt. People often think of the stages as lasting weeks or months. They forget that the stages are responses to feelings that can last for minutes or hours as we flip in and out of one and then another. We do not enter and leave each individual stage in a linear fashion. We may feel one, then another, and back again to the first one.

   My bargaining began with a series of "if onlys":

- If only I saw it for what it truly was.
- If only I didn't marry him.
- If only I recognized his narcissism.
- If only I listened to my intuition early on.
- If only I realized how insecure he is.
- If only I paid more attention to what he didn't say.
- If only I could have put it all together.
- If only I was smarter.
- If only I listened to my inner voice.

It took many months for me to acknowledge that I needed to forgive myself for my harshness at myself for not being able discern who he truly was. My role was the fact that I trusted and made every effort to make the marriage happy.

I have learned that these types of people do not change regardless of how much effort is placed into making it work. I didn't realize this when I was in it, though.

4. *Depression:* After bargaining, our attention moves squarely into the present. Empty feelings present themselves, and grief enters our lives on a deeper level, deeper than we ever imagined. This depressive stage feels as though it will last forever. It's important to understand that this depression is not a sign of mental illness. It's normal to feel depressed when we experience loss. We are sad, and we feel pain on a physical, emotional, spiritual, and intellectual level. It is the appropriate response to a great loss. We withdraw from life, left in a fog of intense sadness, wondering, perhaps, if there is any point in going on alone. Why go on at all? Depression after a loss is too often seen as unnatural: a state to be fixed, something to

snap out of. The first question to ask yourself is whether the situation you're in is actually depressing. The loss of a marriage is a very depressing situation, and depression is a normal and appropriate response. When this loss fully settles in the depths of your soul, of course it is understandably depressing. If grief is a process of healing, then depression is one of the many necessary steps along the way. When the depression lasts over a month, it may be helpful to talk with your physician about possible medication to help with coping. Medication is not the end-all, however. There is a time and place for medication, and you may or may not decide it is appropriate for you. It can help raise the serotonin levels, which in turn will help lower your depressive symptoms.

Throughout my depression, I knew I was blessed with support. I could pick up the phone and call any of my friends at any time. They were incredibly supportive, and because of them, I knew I could get through this harrowing time. Also, every time the thought of him entered my mind, I would say, "Don't go there," and I would shift to a pleasant visualization. It helped. I would question: Why me? This is a loss of a dream. I dream I thought I had—commitment, love, sharing my later years with someone who I thought loved me. All I did was love and care, I thought. I had not connected the dots about narcissistic personality disorder, and that was what I was facing. My married life as I grew to know it was over. I was returning to being a single woman again. Being single was not a bad thing, yet I had lived most of my life being single. Marriage to me was an expansion, a gift that was abruptly taken away. I was so disappointed that he strung me along regarding intensive couples counseling. I told him up front that we had to go to counseling and he continued to stall from November to December, then he said maybe by the end of April! I knew he wasn't interested in saving the marriage, and that was one of the most depressing episodes. He didn't care because he had his supply of attention with the other women. How tragic. I felt helpless, and there was nothing I could do at this point to save the marriage. I had to ask myself, why would I want to?

This is where mindfulness came in. I had to realize it was critical to live moment to moment. Going out into the future was too anxiety provoking. If I did that, I felt totally out of control. While I journaled about my sadness, I also wrote about a game plan to move forward. I knew he would drag it out and never file for divorce because he would look like the bad guy, and image was everything to him. I filed, and knew that if I spoke my truth that good would prevail. It didn't matter that his worshipers idolized him while he played the victim card. I knew I had to get out.

Once I made the decision, it was all about moving onward and upward. I went No Contact.

5. *Acceptance:* This stage is the last of the grief stages. Acceptance is often confused with the notion of being "all right" or "OK" with what has happened. This is not the case. Most people don't ever feel OK or all right about going through the loss of a divorce, at least initially. Most people see the dissolution of their marriage as a failure. I would rather reflect and see it as a learning experience. I don't believe in failure. This stage is about accepting the reality that it's over and recognizing that this new reality is the permanent reality. Our life will never be the same. The hopes, dreams, and expectations of a forever commitment are forever gone. We will never like this reality or make

it OK, but eventually we accept it. We learn to live with it. It is the new norm with which we must learn to live. We must try to live now in a world that is not the same as it once was. Some resist this new norm; however, in time, through bits and pieces of acceptance, we see that we cannot maintain the past intact. It's not just time that heals, it's what we do with the time. Life has been forever changed, and we must readjust to a new life. We must learn to reorganize roles—reassign them to others or take them on ourselves.

Finding acceptance may be just having more good days than bad ones. As we begin to live again and enjoy our life, we continue to heal. We can learn how to make new connections, new meaningful relationships, new interdependencies. Instead of denying our feelings, we listen to our needs; we move, we change, we grow, we evolve. We may start to reach out to others and become involved in their lives. We invest in our friendships and in our relationship with ourselves. We begin to live again, but we cannot do so until we have given grief its time.

I honestly can say that my acceptance came many months after my divorce was final. I thought I had come to acceptance, yet when my lawyer called and told me I was no longer married, it was a mix of emotions from thank goodness to such sadness and a feeling of it being so surreal and knowing I had been replaced. I kept telling myself it was a hard lesson learned and I will be better off. Yet, emotionally, I was so sad. I was alone, yet I was alone throughout most of my marriage.

A couple of weeks after the divorce was final I went to an annual retreat weekend on stress management. A good friend and colleague facilitated the retreat. I realized part of my sadness was that I had a trigger. One year earlier on that exact weekend, I was at the retreat and my husband left to return to Florida "to go back to work." I had an ongoing pit in my stomach since that day. I knew. Three weeks later when I returned to Florida, I saw his appointment book with her name and only her name on the appointment calendar, every day of the week, no one else. It all came flooding back. Triggers can bring unresolved trauma from the subconscious to your conscious awareness and wreak havoc on your psyche. This trauma weaved in and out through the holidays as I returned to Florida to be with my family and I saw him on the road daily going to and from his new girlfriend's house. Newly divorced and having women the entire time he was married, why wouldn't he have women now? I wanted to vomit, because he was in the "honeymoon stage." I knew I was not healed.

Pretty revealing that some people are so insecure, needy and desperate, they cannot be alone for a moment. I found out from a friend of this new woman he was having an affair with her, too, while he was still married to me and she lied about it. After that initial trip back to the Island post divorce, I began asking the Universe to please keep him away from me for subsequent trips. I have returned to Florida over 10 times since, and I have yet to see him. Yes, prayers are answered. Now when I return to the Island I feel so free, and I know that the Universe will keep him at bay. In the unlikely event I ever run into him, it's okay because as of now, I've reached acceptance and I'm happily free.

In trauma, we go through grief and loss. We have to grieve to heal. Grieving is healing.

There is no good, bad, right, or wrong when it comes to grieving. For some it takes months; for others it takes years to complete the grief process. One does not "get over" a loss of such magnitude; however, one does heal and eventually come to a place of acceptance. We weave in and out of grief stages, and some take longer to work through than others.

On the stress scale, death is noted as the highest stressor and worst loss; divorce comes in second. Some people who have divorced feel that it is more difficult than a death because the ex-spouse is still out there. Death is final.

"THERE IS NO SUCH THING AS A PROBLEM WITHOUT A GIFT FOR YOU IN ITS HANDS. YOU SEEK PROBLEMS BECAUSE YOU NEED THEIR GIFTS."
—RICHARD BACH

CHAPTER THREE

NARCISSISM: THE SPECTRUM

As a clinician for many years, I was aware of narcissistic personality disorder (NPD) from my training and NPD criteria from the *Diagnostic and Statistical Manual of Mental Disorders*, 5th edition (*DSM-5*). I will cover the entire spectrum of narcissism in this chapter, which ranges from mere traits of narcissism to NPD and extreme narcissism.

Now more than ever with social media, posting photos of self, self, and self, it's no wonder we social media buffs may be a little (or a lot) narcissistic. Just like with the empath (discussed later in this chapter), narcissism runs on a spectrum. There is a healthy component of narcissism, but let me be clear, the narcissism I will describe in most of this chapter is unhealthy narcissism (i.e., NPD and extreme narcissism). Healthy narcissism is caring about oneself, but not to the degree of total self-absorption. Most of us want to have healthy self-esteem—to believe that we are worthy, to have a nice-looking appearance, and to maintain a good sense of self. It's when the self-absorption becomes so intense that an individual lacks caring and empathy for others that we look at narcissistic traits and beyond.

Who Is the Narcissist?

He or she can be a spouse, co-worker, parent, friend, or neighbor. The term "narcissistic" can be used to describe everything from a social media buff who's a little self-absorbed to a full-blown narcissistic personality disorder, which is a diagnosis from the *DSM-5*, to extreme (malignant) narcissism.

Individuals who meet the criteria for narcissistic personality disorder (NPD) are diagnosed clinically with a personality disorder. Personality disorders do not change. The grain of our wood is set by age five. Behavior can change, yet when one is diagnosed with a personality disorder, change is probably not going to occur. People with NPD also generally have traits of antisocial personality disorder (ASPD), and it is common for an overlap to occur in these two types of disorders. For people with these disorders, manipulation and control are primary traits within relationships, because they are masters at deceit, exploitation, and lies.

If you are in a relationship with someone I just described, you cannot begin a recovery program while in this kind of abusive relationship. You can only heal when you end it, because you have no way to defend yourself. Because of the cognitive dissonance, you dislike this person for what he or she has done and you are raging with anger toward him or her, as well as toward yourself for not seeing it. Yet, you also feel as though you love the narcissist on some level because of the "good times" you had. You have experienced a loss—a loss of an opportunity, of what you thought was going to be a healthy, happy existence with someone you loved. It wasn't real to him or her, but it was so real to you. Don't be afraid or ashamed to say you loved this person. Discovering this person was not who you thought he or she was felt like a death. Although you may think you lost, you didn't—you won if you got out.

The *DSM-5* (American Psychiatric Association, 2013) has a list of criteria for NPD that includes at least five of the following:

1. Has a grandiose sense of self-importance (e.g., exaggerates achievements and talents, expects to be recognized as superior without commensurate achievements).
2. Is preoccupied with fantasies of unlimited success, power, brilliance, beauty, or ideal love.
3. Believes that he or she is "special" and unique and can be only understood by, or should associate with, other special or high status people (or institutions).
4. Requires excessive admiration.
5. Has a sense of entitlement (i.e., unreasonable expectations or especially favorable treatment or automatic compliance with his or her expectations).
6. Is interpersonally exploitative (i.e., takes advantage of others to achieve his or her own ends).
7. Lacks empathy, is unwilling to recognize or identify with the feelings and needs of others.
8. Is often envious of others or believes that others are envious of him or her.
9. Shows arrogant, haughty behaviors or attitudes.

These criteria give an overview of NPD. What I will disclose in this book is more complex than the above criteria, however, especially when it comes to relationships and how narcissists exploit them and leave their victims reeling with devastation and betrayal that may take years to recover from.

Narcissism is a spectrum disorder. Remember that the more traits an individual has, the deeper the betrayal and wounding the partner will experience. The following sections describe the two main types of narcissists, overt and covert.

The Overt Narcissist

Although a narcissist is a narcissist and they have the same core traits, the overt narcissist (ON) is outwardly entitled, aggressive, annoying, and pushy. They are extremely suave while they use their charm. They love bomb and try to impress someone in order to get what they are seeking, and they will be quick to let others know how great they are while lacking any empathy. My biological father was an overt narcissist. He could be nasty and treat others with a sense of entitlement and arrogance, and belittle them while going on and on about himself and how great he was.

He was horribly entitled, especially in a restaurant (Don't you know who I am?), self-absorbed, selfish, in it for his own personal gain, a pathological liar, a cheater, and a "look at me I'm great" type. I observed him being verbally abusive to his father and speaking horribly about his brother, who was a priest, and sister, who was a kind, loving human being. As a child, I was given so many unfulfilled promises about what he was going to give me. When push came to shove, his recurring line was, "Hon, if I had it, you know I would give it to you." This became more evident as I entered college and not once, through undergraduate, graduate, or doctorate school, did he contribute, yet my aunt told me of stories he would tell his so-called friends, that he "put me though college." He wouldn't even help me pay back any of my school loans over the years. I do remember clearly that after

I graduated from college, he said, "Just because you went to college, don't think you have the world by the ass." He never attended college. He went from job to job and was unemployed more than employed.

I always thought something seemed strange about his behavior, yet at that age, I wasn't able to wrap my brain around who he really was. ONs will be the first to let you know about how connected they are to the high and mighty, whether they are celebrities, political figures, or well-known community leaders. Unfortunately, there are so many political leaders who are ONs all the way to the top. They will never apologize for their wrong-doing. My father was an alcoholic, had an affair while my mother was pregnant with me, and told her he could not decide which woman he wanted, the other woman or my mother. Good thing my mother decided for him!

Overt narcissists are a bit easier to detect as they are outright brash classic narcissist and act courageous even though they are not at the core of their being. This type can blow up over something just to prove a point and adamantly try to convince you that he or she is right. Thus, they are terrified and have much shame and trauma—they just act it out. They believe they are superior. An overt narcissist can get right in your face and totally turn you off immediately. The ON would be more likely to have been raised by an entitled narcissist who was smart, extroverted, and filled with entitlement and never learned healthy boundaries. The ON is also likely to be the golden child. They never learned empathy because they are the classic narcissist who thinks they are one of the elite and privileged. They are above anyone else, including the law or medicine, and can be in these professions along with being in politics or CEOs of companies. The ON will never let you see their vulnerability. They will act as though there is never anything wrong with them.

"THE MOMENT PEOPLE REMEMBER THAT THEY'VE FORGOTTEN IS A MOMENT OF GRACE."
—BARBARA DE ANGELIS

The Covert Narcissist

This type of narcissist is also considered passive-aggressive. A covert narcissist (CN) is, in my opinion, the more malignant of the two types. They also lack empathy—they just pretend they have it. I was married to a covert narcissist; therefore, there was a blind spot to the world I was about to enter. What I discovered about the covert narcissist is the hidden aspects of their dark side; however, when their mask begins to slip, look out, it's not pretty. The covert narcissist is all about image. They want to be well thought of (pillars of the community). They usually are liked and respected, unlike overt narcissists. ONs can be annoying, pushy, extravagantly grandiose, and even flashy as they brag about who they are and what they have, especially in terms of their material goods and their looks. They make grandiose remarks about all of their accomplishments, as if no one else could compare. Remember, they are charming as well, and have an air of superiority. ONs are not liked after people see them for who they really are. These types tend to have shorter-term marriages and relationships. In contrast, CNs can have long-term marriages, and their spouses do not truly understand they are married to a narcissist for many years. I also believe that generationally, the couples of the 1960s didn't really understand if one partner was a narcissist. I have seen couples from that generation where one partner became very ill or even died from an illness or disease. Years of narcissistic abuse from a spouse can wear on the individual being abused. Emotional abuse can be just as damaging as physical abuse.

This takes its toll on the physical body, and I have known of cases in my counseling practice where women became sick because they lived with a narcissist for many years and finally succumbed to illness.

Nowadays, because we are learning so much more about this personality disorder, partners who become ill can get out once they realize they have lived with this deceit, manipulation, secretiveness, lying, control, and facade for many years. The question is, will they? It is very difficult once they become trauma bonded, but it's not impossible. Some partners fear being alone, especially if they were married for many years and if the narcissist is the bread winner; they don't feel they can make it on their own. I know of one woman who is in a long-term marriage to a narcissist and although she wants to leave him, she is afraid because he has her convinced she would be on the street. He is a multimillionaire.

"TALK ABOUT ME GOOD, TALK ABOUT ME BAD, JUST TALK ABOUT ME."
—CHRISTIANE NORTHRUP, M.D.

A covert narcissist can be a physician, lawyer, community leader, minister, therapist, head of an organization that helps others, and pillar of the community who presents as a very genuine, caring, kind human being—a humanitarian if you will. They are masterful at living a lie. It is common for them to have careers where they are in a position of authority. Why not? They want to be in control and to be seen as an authority in their field. They love to impress others with their expertise. Now, this does not mean that every professional who is in a position of authority is a CN or ON. There are wonderful, real authentic professionals who are good and are not in professions to be anything else but helpful to others. The difference is that the CNs are all about themselves, but they pretend that they're not. Their false self pretends it's all about you, when in fact, they could care less about you. They can paint a picture of how much they care, even be a great caretaker of you if you are ill and act all humble. It's all an act. It's just not real. They can hide their true tortured self for decades, if not forever. CNs do have just as grandiose a sense of self as the ONs; however, they can hide behind the kind, caring, interested in you, great listener facade, so you won't see that they only see you as an object, and any interest they appear to have in you is for their own personal gain. They are so good at manipulating you that you won't even notice how the attention goes back to them; you'll only begin to perceive something's odd when you find yourself realizing something doesn't "feel" right, but you can't put your finger on it. I look back and remember thinking that a lot, and I just didn't know what it was. Then I would think that maybe I said something or did something to provoke him into being cold and aloof, withdrawn, and giving silent treatments. Often partners of CNs will feel this way and end up apologizing for something they did not do, but felt they did.

What is so puzzling about a covert narcissist is they generally don't yell, become physical, or threaten; this is what makes them covert. This can be utterly confusing to the partner, because it's emotional abuse and so hidden. The impact this type of abuse has on the victim is profound, much more than anyone could ever know unless they have lived it. There are no physical scars; however, the emotional wounds run deep and take many years to heal. A victim of this type of abuse may feel depressed, anxious, sad, lonely, unappreciated, unloved, worthless, useless, inadequate, and as though something is deeply wrong with them. I remember feeling confused at times, and I couldn't pinpoint what the confusion was about. It eluded me, yet something was off. I remember saying to myself many times, "Damned if I do, and damned if I don't." Nothing I could do ever felt right, just like when I was around my father. As a child, I had that same feeling with him, so that would trigger when I felt this way as an adult in the marriage.

You may wonder why the narcissist came into your life. For me, it goes back to my childhood with my biological father, whom I refer to throughout this book. My parents divorced when I was two years old, and I subconsciously carried the wounds with me through adulthood. Those wounds re-entered my world anytime I was around my biological father, which was once or twice a year.

When I was 30 years old, I went to therapy for some personal issues I needed to address, and it was a part of my doctoral program. My therapist delved deep with me regarding my developmental stages and what I could remember taking place from my earliest memory. After many months, her persistence paid off in helping me understand how blocked I was with regard to the overt abuse of my father and how it was affecting my relationships with men. She was right. I had a series of these relationships and unconsciously selected narcissistic types.

I was attracted to narcissistic men, no doubt about it. I thought I had a real handle on it because I didn't marry any of them for 53 years. Wow, I managed to hold off making a mistake, lucky me. In the beginning of each relationship I would say to myself, "I finally broke the cycle. This one is great." Then after a few months, each partner's true colors would shine through, and it was a repetitive cycle for me. They were either emotionally unavailable or an alcoholic or both! With the husband, I thought to myself, "Yay, I broke the cycle, he's not an alcoholic!" What I neglected and "forgot" to see was covert narcissism.

What I can tell you is that narcissists love chaos. They seem to have a keen sense that their partners are either wounded, broken, or an empath. They are parasites and latch onto those who are compassionate, friendly, trusting, attractive, and have either a successful career or money.

The main focus of a narcissist is getting supply in the form of adoration and attention from anyone and everyone. They pretend to love and act as though they will take care of you, especially if they get you to marry them. The real truth is that they cannot survive without doing damage to the ones they pretend to love. Once the devaluing occurs, you can bet they already have someone else they are love bombing. They will do the same thing to the new person. The new ones haven't the slightest idea what's going on either, and I guarantee you, even if the narcissist lives with or marries them, he or she will do the exact same thing to them as he or she did to you.

The reason narcissists don't care is because they do not have the capacity to bond emotionally. Depending on where you are in the process, I would recommend you continue to educate yourself through this book and get out while you can. If you choose to stay, you will wind up in a vicious cycle and wonder what has happened to you.

One thing I want to stress is that being with an ON or a CN in a relationship is *not* normal. No abuse is normal, regardless of how overtly physical or subtle. It's unacceptable, and there is absolutely no excuse for it, ever. I also want to emphasize that when you are with a healthy partner, you are not thinking about such words as *toxic, narcissist, abuse, deceit, secretive, liar, cold, aloof, silent treatments, devalue, discard, gaslighting, manipulative, control, cheater, selfish, annoying, delusional,* or *confused,* to name a few. You are thinking about how this person is in alignment with what they say and how they behave. There is a consistency and continuity with follow-through. It feels good to be around this person.

> "HE WHO KNOWS OTHERS IS WISE, BUT HE WHO KNOWS HIMSELF IS ENLIGHTENED. HE WHO OVERCOMES OTHERS IS STRONG, BUT HE WHO OVERCOMES HIMSELF IS MIGHTIER STILL."
>
> —LAO-TZU

The Signs of Narcissistic Abuse

There is a belief in our culture that narcissists are those who are into taking selfies. It has become quite the buzzword, especially in the last few years with certain leaders who are thought of as narcissists. Yet, most don't know that narcissism goes much deeper. I believe narcissism begins early on in life when there is shame, self-doubt, and emotional neglect. An empty hole remains in the human while he or she covers the hole up with psychological defenses. These defenses remain as the person grows into adulthood and only knows conditional love. This conditional love is based on a condition that you will love me only if I meet your expectations. When these expectations of others are not met, then the unworthiness sets in, the vicious cycle of emptiness continues, and the person remains a tortured soul.

The following sections describe six signs that you're in a relationship with a narcissist and experiencing abuse.

1. There Is Something "Off" in Your Relationship

Something just doesn't seem right; rather, it seems off. Maybe you feel confused and feel your partner did something that he or she should apologize for and he or she doesn't. Some of your discussions or arguments get twisted, and it always becomes your fault and there is no ownership on their part. Perhaps you want to get together with some of your friends for a bite to eat and your partner gives you the cold shoulder or makes you feel guilty for leaving them at home. You worry the entire evening about them, and when you get home they give you the silent treatment. A normal partner with good character would tell you to have a wonderful time and say hello to your friends from him or her.

Perhaps you put up with the name calling, or the verbally or physically abusive behavior. Yes, silent treatments are abusive and punishing as well. If you do tolerate any of this behavior, you have to ask yourself, why? What is it within you that keeps you tolerating it: fear, insecurity, low self-worth, or just lack of boundary setting? If you don't set healthy boundaries, then chances are you are feeling one of the above about yourself.

2. You Give Up Pieces of Yourself to Keep the Relationship Alive

Remember that it's all about them. They can and do easily manipulate you to give up things you may want to have or do to acquiesce to them. In fact, they expect it. They may get bent out of shape over something that normal partners wouldn't think twice about. Some narcissists will be the passive-aggressive types, whereas others will be explosive, depending on their anger style. They all believe they are entitled and superior, and they will let you know it.

Narcissists like being served in all capacities. Think about it: When did your partner ever offer to do something for you from a place of pure unconditional love? If they do anything for you, it's from a place of "What can you do for me?" You most likely will find yourself bending over backward to please your partner, and any expense will fall to you.

You may also find that you would like to discuss certain things with your partner; however, you worry that you will be chastised or devalued, so you decide not to mention anything. Maybe you have a fear that this person will leave you, and you begin to act out of your own comfort zone and do anything to prevent this. This is giving up pieces of yourself to the place where you have no self. When you find yourself walking on eggshells, that is when you have lost pieces of yourself. You find yourself making all kinds of effort to please your partner, but to no avail, and the rabbit hole gets deeper and deeper.

In my marriage, nothing I could do would please my husband. Nothing. I could turn myself into a pretzel and bend to just about any shape to please, and it never did. I didn't move on the tennis court, I was a fat mama, I couldn't cook, so he ate frozen dinners and refused the food I prepared for him. I walked unnaturally, and on and on the criticisms came. Enabling behavior can be an unconscious way to perpetuate the abusive behavior because he knows he's got you hooked.

3. You Are Not Your True, Authentic Self

After my divorce, my childhood friend, who has known me for more than 50 years, said, "You are back to your old self." How revealing was that? I had given away pieces of myself without even realizing it. When we are not being our authentic selves because we are trying to please and gain approval from our partner, something is amiss. You can always take pride in being your true, authentic self. Remember, it's the narcissist that wears the mask of the false self. My friends saw this in me. I knew at some point, yet I was lost then. It wasn't worth it to me to argue with him because it would just be another silent treatment for days. I finally learned to just go about my business and take care of myself within the marriage, or so I thought.

It really did get the best of me, though. In reflection, I am sure that I behaved in ways that I would not have in a normal relationship. I even found myself more angry than usual because I rarely was angry, but he told me how much rage I had. Rage? Seriously? I never thought of myself as rageful; however, because he would regularly say that, he knew it fueled me, and of course I became angry. I know now that he brought out the worst in me rather than the best. There was rarely laughter in our home; it seemed to always be so serious. I believe laughter is necessary in every household. If there is no laughter on a regular basis, what is there? What's really going on? Please know that when you are enmeshed with an unhealthy, toxic person, you will get sick.

I know without a doubt that if I would have stayed, I would have become sick.

4. You Begin to Question Yourself as a Good Human Being

Narcissists are notorious at using an unconscious defense mechanism called projection. When they use projection, they are projecting onto you what is really going on with them. For instance, if your partner tells you that you are lying, cheating, or something similar, then that is what he or she is doing. They are merely projecting that onto you. Remember, narcissists take no accountability, so it's very common for them to use this tactic to take any of the guilt away from themselves. Once I was onto his projection, I began to understand that he either had or wanted these things for himself (i.e., a rich woman, money, status, influence). He projected all of those things onto me. Because of my narcissistic father, at times I did question my self-worth, as I had since I was very young. The things my father projected onto me as a child were ridiculous; however, as I child, I couldn't grasp it all. I do remember a time when I was only six years old and his second wife said to me, "You need to spend more time with your father." I remember thinking, but he's always on the golf course, so how can I spend more time with him? Even though a part of me knew that was a selfish statement his wife made to me, it still made me question my self-worth. Dad doesn't think I'm good enough because I don't spend enough time with him. Often this low self-esteem starts early in life because of unhealthy treatment by a parent.

Remember, narcissists lack empathy and integrity. They usually lie, cheat, and thrive on creating drama and getting a dose or supply of the partner's attention and adoration. Don't be the supplier any longer.

5. There Are No Healthy Boundaries

When you are in a relationship with a narcissist, healthy boundary setting is paramount. When someone comes from a family of dysfunction, usually there were no healthy boundaries in that household, so many empaths didn't learn how to set any boundaries, much less healthy ones. I hear many partners who were or are with narcissists say they never learned how to set boundaries.

When setting boundaries, you are telling someone how far they can go with you. You most likely will be tested if you attempt to set a boundary, but if you learn to stick to it and follow through, you will be able to feel stronger and more empowered, and this will help you to rise to resilience.

6. The Addiction to Security Is the Biggest Cause of Insecurity

Addiction happens with narcissists. It seems absurd to be addicted to someone who treats us like we would never consciously want to be treated. So what is this about?

It has to do with trauma bonding and physiological conditions happening within your nervous system. You are definitely out of sorts when you are feeling manic and hooking back up with the narcissist who betrayed you. Or when you are away from this person you cannot function or think clearly. It truly is addictive, and it's hard to break an addiction.

This requires trauma work from a professional. You could be suffering from anxiety, depression, an autoimmune disease, or a multitude of other physically and emotionally depleting illnesses. Deep inner subconscious healing and shifting needs to occur so you feel like you can move forward without being gripped by someone who doesn't even care for you.

Chances are you are also feeling symptoms of abuse. Be it verbal, physical, sexual, or all three, you most likely feel posttraumatic stress and are in need of self-soothing techniques to help you get your power back and keep it rather than giving it away. Giving your power away is a volatile thing to do and leaves you with nothing, no self, and caught in a vicious cycle of shame.

Know that you cannot ever give up; however, you can let go. Let go of the horrible treatment you received; let go of the shame you've been left with; let go of having no sense of self; let go of living a life of being controlled, manipulated, lied to, cheated on, used, and abused.

Seeing the Narcissist for Who He or She Is

Do you think you would be able to spot a narcissist if he or she was around you? This is where the empath can get into trouble. From what you just read, you now know that an empath has many gifts, but challenges arise when the empath gets hooked up with the narcissist (i.e., energy vampire). The key to what a narcissist needs is a supply of adoration, attention, sex, worship and often financial support from his partner. As long as the narcissist is getting plenty of supply, he or she thrives on the attention. Once the supply begins to dwindle, they will go on to the next source. Just like the vampire needs a blood supply to sustain life, the narcissist needs to keep the supply going to sustain the emptiness inside.

Based on the empath's belief system, it's no wonder they feel they can heal anyone they care about. It's ingrained. It's our temperament. We as empaths reject that others can become so cold, aloof, punishing, calculating, and lacking in the empathy department. We will believe that something is wrong with us before we will see the deficits in our flawed partners. The paradox with empaths is that, as intuitive as they are, they fail to listen to what their intuitive voice tells them from the get-go. Remember the poppies? They pop up everywhere, and what do we empaths do? We ignore them because we don't want to see those flaws because if we paid attention to them, we would be forced to leave the narcissist and be alone. Yet, if we could just see that growth can occur from learning this painful lesson, we can thrive and rise to resilience.

Narcissists are known to have "empathy-deficient disorder." Narcissists seek out empaths for their incredible energy, compassion, giving, caring, empathy, and natural tendency to uplift and share all they have for the greater good. They want what we have, but they cannot and will not ever get it. They want our energy.

So why do empaths get into relationships with narcissists? It all goes back to our old wounds, the beliefs we derive from them, and the developmental stages of life. Unconsciously, we may feel unworthy of love, caring, and giving, so we do all of the giving so someone, namely our partner, in the hope that they will love and care for us.

Often, it's an unconscious selection process whereby we reach out in partnership to work through the issues of our parent or parents from which we are trying to heal. In this process, we feel unlovable, and we hide our own vulnerabilities to not feel or be rejected. We are always looking out for a way to get approval and prove ourselves. In this, we hide our true selves, like the narcissist, but the difference is we give and they take because they cover up their wounds with defenses and we wear our hearts on our sleeves.

Another reason we stay in bad relationships is because we want to be accepted and not hurt others' feelings. We believe the narcissist will feel the same way, too. But that's not going to happen…ever. Narcissists do not change. Narcissists will use and abuse you and suck the life force out of you until you are broken in mind, body, spirit, and emotions. By hiding our vulnerabilities to avoid rejection, we shut down. Old soul empaths are especially attracted to narcissists because they are self-confident, energetic, and have incredible empathy in the goodness of all people. Old soul empaths believe essentially everyone is good and see the Divine parts in them that they themselves see in everyone. They believe that their love and caring can heal everyone. Unfortunately, it cannot. If you are in a relationship with a narcissist, you have to come to terms with seeing it for what it is, not the potential for what you think it could be; otherwise, you will stay mired in the wounds of your past. This is a huge lesson for most of us. And if we fail to see it for what it is, the vicious cycle continues.

Narcissists seek out the empaths who are likely to put up with their tactics. They do know exactly what they are doing. They use and exploit for their own personal gain to the detriment of the empath. One of the narcissist's greatest defense mechanisms is the use of projection onto their victims. They are also good at rationalizing and justifying their actions.

My concern is that I am seeing this problem growing in my counseling practice. It seems that young female adults are coming in with broken hearts and feeling so wounded that they are suffering from narcissistic abuse. Not that males don't have this happen to them—I have worked with broken-hearted men—but I am noticing it happening more to women. I am grateful that women are seeking out counseling to help them understand they were with a narcissist. I reassure them that although they are in great pain, they can and will heal. We work through the betrayal, deceit, and all of the symptoms they encounter, while working through grief and loss. I explain why no contact is necessary—or minimal contact if they work together or have children. This can and will expedite the healing process. I also help them learn where they are on the empath spectrum and how narcissists (especially the covert narcissists) seek out certain types of people. Narcissists choose targets who are kind, trusting, genuine, vulnerable, nurturing, loving beings. They can pick them out in an instant. Plus, empaths give out those kind, compassionate signals, and the narcissists pick up on them immediately. We are magnets.

Perhaps this phenomenon is growing because of the Me Too movement. More people are speaking out than ever before, and it is no longer swept under the rug like it used to be. More and more reports of abuse and domestic violence are being reported due to the increased awareness of narcissistic abuse.

Narcissists may think they are above it all; however, I believe the time is now for us to stand in the light and no longer tolerate the senselessness of any kind of misrepresentation of honor and respect for humankind.

Love Lies

With regard to our brain, we now know through research that rejection, heartache, abandonment, and betrayal travel along the same familiar pathways that produce physical pain. It's every bit as painful as a physical blow to the body. Getting past an intimate betrayal involves oxytocin being eliminated from our pleasure center. It's similar to an addict going cold turkey off of heroin. We get the hits of oxytocin and dopamine when we experience the love bond. When we discover the lies and betrayal, and those hits are no longer there, we go into emotional and biochemical withdrawal.

Despite what the betraying partner did, we know that the rejected partner, especially in the beginning of the very vulnerable state, is experiencing feelings of longing that are excruciating to the point of nonfunctionality. It's normal to think of your partner at least 85% of the time and yearn to reunite with him or her. Think of a small child being abandoned and placed in an orphanage where he or she knows no one. This orphaned child wants to connect and bond with his or her primary caregiver, the parent, yet the parent is gone. This longing and yearning is at the core of betrayal. This sense of powerlessness brings on distress to the core of one's being.

I can attest that most likely the person who betrayed because of his or her own emptiness and insecurity has already planned in advance to get a new supply of adoration and attention when his or her attention from you is running low. It could be from someone they knew they could get it from because it was easy (not because they fell in love) and they are not thinking about you, but rather their new victim because it's new and fresh and they can get all the supply they want. They are too weak to be put through their own biochemical withdrawal, so they easily replace you.

"WHO LOOKS OUTSIDE, DREAMS. WHO LOOKS INSIDE, AWAKENS."
—CARL JUNG

What Type of Individual Attracts a Narcissist?

In my depths of soul searching as to what went wrong, it didn't take me long to realize my role in this marriage. I thought (consciously, at least) that I had broken the cycle of attracting unavailable men. You know, the ones who are not there for you emotionally. The men I attracted throughout my adult life mostly were self-absorbed and not able to emotionally commit because they were either alcoholic, jobless, self-absorbed, or just plain not interested in commitment. I discovered later that the manipulation, control, lies, and deception went over my head, at least initially. My denial lasted until it became blatant, when I began to discover the written evidence.

I started reading all I could on the spectrum of empaths. An empath is defined as a highly sensitive individual who absorbs the energy of others. Empaths are highly intuitive and caring. They have a permeable nervous system and hyperactive reflexes. They have the ability to experience everything, pleasure and pain—sometimes to an extreme. They are super-responders: they have a heightened sensory experience of a relationship. They are very attuned to people (at times even telepathically), and they have a kinship with nature. They can be exceptionally responsive lovers. The challenge of being an empath is they are sponges and absorb everything (not always to their own benefit). They can unknowingly absorb people's stress into their own bodies. They often become overloaded, anxious, and exhausted. This differs from ordinary empathy, such as when you empathize with a friend's break-up with her boyfriend or celebrating your parents' 50th anniversary. Your heart goes out to others whether it's a joyful or sorrowful occasion. Relationship empathy goes much further. You merge with your partner and actually feel his or her joys and fears as if they were your own. Thus, romantic relationships, specifically live-in ones, can be challenging without clear boundaries and communication.

Empaths have a tendency to use drugs or overeat to drown their sensitivities. When an empath sees a physician for various issues from having absorbed the energy of others, the typical western-trained physician is not going to understand the empath's issues; therefore, it is likely that the physician will prescribe medication. Most likely, this is not what the empath needs. The empath needs someone who is knowledgeable in who they are and how they operate. Medications will just "medicate" the issue and not get to the real gifts and strengths of the empath. What they do need is the understanding of what's going on with them and how to use healthy coping techniques and protect sensitivities while learning to express genuine authentic needs and take charge rather than becoming a victim and running from their true selves.

Empaths are prone to going into health professions, which is no surprise because they are givers and genuinely care for others. They make great healthcare providers until they take on too much, don't set boundaries, and burn out. This is all too common.

My Experience as an Empath

I knew that from childhood I was highly sensitive and reveled in alone time, and I thought I was different from the other children. I was especially sensitive in the Catholic elementary school I attended because I was the only child in the class whose parents were divorced. I felt shame and embarrassment, and I was made fun of. I tried to get the attention of the nuns, only to be pushed aside. When I played by myself, I had to be outside as much as possible. My grandfather once asked, "Are you an indoor girl or an outdoor girl?" Without hesitation, I always replied that I was an outdoor girl. I am to this day.

I used to take the tin pans from chicken pot pies and dig in the earth and make mud pies. I would climb trees and ride my bicycle down steep hills, and I walked a lot with my uncle as a child. I was alone a lot of the time, and it wasn't until high school that I became more extraverted. Through my adulthood and being on the cusp of introversion/extraversion, I came to realize that regardless of how social I was, I needed rest and rejuvenation to return to wholeness and balance. This is where nature is my solace. I cannot think of a place I would rather be than in nature. I have always felt this way; however, I feel it now more than ever. I enjoy going to the city for shows, conferences, and great music; however, after a couple of days, I get the itch to return home to my country life. I only lived in a city once, and I was a young adult. It was fun in many ways, yet I felt a sense of being trapped because there was no nature around. It was so concrete and big. I remember saying that this was a place for me to hang my hat. I lived in the city for six years, and then was called to Sanibel Island in Florida, where I lived for 25 years. There was and still is nature there, including beautiful beaches with lovely unique seashells that wash upon the shoreline. I loved being an "island girl" for many years, yet there was another calling: the mountains.

I was called to a place where I still live today. I find it to be one of the most beautiful and majestic places on this earth. I feel incredibly blessed to live where there are four seasons, each carrying its own essence of magical beauty. I have never felt such a freedom, loving the landscape and the feeling of embracing all that I have here. Perhaps my empath gifts and sensitivities have shown me this is where I feel at home more than any other place I have lived.

The Empath Spectrum and Types of Empaths

Best-selling author Judith Orloff, M.D., authored a book, *The Empath's Survival Guide: Life Strategies for Sensitive People*. This book helped me understand myself and realize what I always knew subconsciously: I am an empath. I just didn't know the name for someone like me. As a therapist, being in the helping/service profession, I knew I had special and natural gifts, which is what empaths have. When I took the quiz in Dr. Orloff's book, I realized I am an empath high on the spectrum with my own set of gifts and challenges.

Along the spectrum of being an empath, the ordinarily sensitive person who wants to stay open-hearted and avoid compassion fatigue and burnout needs to learn the skills to protect themselves yet still be contributing to the planet. That is one end of the spectrum. The other end is being a full-blown empath. This end of the spectrum is an empath who does not have the same defenses or energy filters that the rest of the population has. They tend to take other people's feelings into their bodies, become emotional sponges, and become exhausted. This can wear and tear on the physical body and manifest into illness and disease. Some common ailments empaths are susceptible to include adrenal fatigue, migraines, fibromyalgia, autoimmune disease, panic disorder, and agoraphobia. I have had clients who wouldn't go out of their house because it was too overwhelming. In our 24/7, fast-paced culture, empaths are at high risk for burning out.

The following clarifies the spectrum of different types of empaths:

- *Emotional empath:* This is one of the more common types of empaths. An emotional empath may take on the emotional energy of someone who may be feeling joyful or upset. The emotional empath may become overwhelmed, overstimulated, and anxious, and absorb others' stress. So when you are around others and you are feeling a certain emotion, you may want to excuse yourself, be alone somewhere for a few minutes, and see if you are still feeling as though you have picked up someone's energy or if the energy is your own. I was trained many years ago that as a therapist, I have to know how not to take on my clients' energies. Otherwise, I would be a doormat and I would take all of the problems of the day home with me! Although I have empathy and compassion for those who seek my guidance, I know my boundaries and how not to take on others' emotions. Emotional empaths also have a sensitivity to noise, crowds, smells, and excessive talkers, and some even prefer to drive their own car to an event so they can leave when they want to. They may feel as though they don't fit in and need alone time to get restored and rejuvenated.

If you feel like you are an emotional empath, your challenge is to be able to differentiate your emotions from someone else's.

- *Physical empath:* This type of empath is especially attuned to others' physical symptoms and tends to absorb them into their body. They intuitively know what ails another person because they end up taking it on themselves. For example, say your friend gets migraines and you get a migraine, and you are not sure why because you usually never get one. You have taken your friend's migraine into your body. On a more positive note, a physical empath can also become energized by someone's sense of well-being.

  Years ago, I was dating someone who became gravely ill. He was transported to a Denver hospital from Vail due to sepsis. That night, after his parents went to the airport to pick up his brothers, I was alone in his hospital while he lay still with no sign of life. The physician said to me, "He has less than a 10% chance of making it through the night." I remember starting to faint and asked the doctor for a cup of water. What I realized later was that I was taking into my physical body what was happening with him as his body was shutting down. When the doctor left the room, I was alone, standing at his bedside, and something came over me. To this day, I can only come up with the fact that it was divine intervention. Some inner strength came through me and I had a talk with him that came from my heart. That night the priest came in and gave him last rites. We all left and I went back to my hotel and lit candles and did a healing meditation for him. The phone rang at 5:00 a.m., and my heart jumped out of my chest. It was his father telling me that he made it through the night. He was not out of the woods, but after two additional months of being in the hospital, he finally was able to begin a long rehabilitation process, and he is alive today. We do take others' physical energy into our bodies.

- *Intuitive empath:* Tuning in to their intuition allows an intuitive empath to experience extraordinary feelings and perceptions that tend to be heightened. They may get a strong feeling about something that is spot on, or may have a crystal clear dream that confirms something they already know. They may even experience telepathy, messages, and possibly communication with the other side. They can empathically connect to the great mystery. They can also pick up information about someone just by being around them. By using this telepathic gift, they can sense others' thoughts. It is a great gift to have this, especially if someone is not being honest, because you will notice the intentions around them, so then you can set your own healthy boundaries so you won't get caught up in their facade and you will surround yourself with those you feel a healthy connection with.

- *Precognitive empath:* This type of empath can have premonitions about the future while awake or dreaming. You may also refer to them as psychics. This is a gift that some have to help them with what their future has in store.

- *Dream/mediumship empath:* A dream empath has vivid dreams and can receive information about dreams that guides others in their own lives. Mediumship empaths can access spirits on the other side. All mediums are psychics (precognitive), but not all psychics are mediums.

It's beneficial to keep a dream journal. You can piece together dreams and ask questions and even get answers through your dreams. It's best to record your dream when you are in a hypnogogic state, the time between sleep and waking. Before you open your eyes, center yourself. You will then have a much greater chance of remembering your dream and writing it down or recording it. Ask how your dream applies to your life today. Even nightmares can be healing. See what's chasing you in the darkest parts of your soul, then let it go and you will heal.

You can also harmonize with the state of consciousness you travel to as you are in it. You can become one with it. I love working with my dreams. Even though I have what I refer to as "trauma dreams" occasionally, I know that my subconscious is working through what it needs to heal, and it does. I am grateful for my dreams and find them so fascinating and healing as I communicate and travel with various layers of consciousness that we are not aware of in our daily waking state.

- *Plant empath:* People who are plant empaths can feel the needs of plants and connect with their essence. I have never considered myself a plant empath; however, I had an interesting experience with one. When my marriage was falling apart, so was my ficus plant. The leaves had turned yellow and brown. Most of them had fallen to the ground. I was living alone at that time. I decided that perhaps I could save the plant. The next day I went to the nursery, purchased a larger pot, and repotted the plant. I talked with the plant and told her that she can have a rebirth and thrive, even though there were barely any leaves on her. Two years and two moves later, the ficus is back to being a huge plant, and she is shiny and thriving. I am so proud of her and thrilled that she's quite happy sitting by the large picture window getting plenty of sun and care.

- *Earth empath:* Also known as a geomantic empaths, these empaths are centered and grounded to the earth. They are also attuned to the changes going on with our planet, solar system, and weather (i.e., climate change). It's how they feel the universe. These empaths may be connected to certain places such as stones, vortexes, or churches. Earth empaths love being in nature and feel so connected with spirit and even their spirit guides. They also may relate to the history of a sacred place and pick up on the energies such as a certain sadness, exuberance, or grief that may have occurred.

  Have you ever watched the night sky on a beautiful night? I live in the country, and on a clear night the millions of stars just light up the sky, and I actually feel this amazing energy. I have always felt a connection to the earth mother and her beauty wherever I go. Some may also attribute this empathic nature to the earth from previous lifetimes. I have read about people who have had deja vu experiences, feeling strongly they have been to a specific place lifetimes ago.

- *Animal empath:* Animal empaths can connect with the animal population and communicate with them. Many years ago, my amazing veterinarian told me that the animals talk to her, and she has a special communication with them. She was somewhat reluctant to share this with her clients, concerned that they would think she was crazy and would take their pets elsewhere. I encouraged her to tell her patients and that they would embrace her gift. Today she has a three-week waiting list.

There are more pet therapy programs now than ever before, and we know the many healing modalities that pets can perform. Pets work in hospitals with patients, and in prisons (which are full of narcissists, sociopaths, and psychopaths) where these inmates can choose to participate with the pet therapy program. Animal empaths are also involved with animal rescue. I take my yellow lab Archie to the local hospital monthly, and I cannot emphasize the joy in the patients' (and staff's) eyes when they have a sweet four-legged soul walk into the room with a wagging tail and such presence.

- *Food empath:* Although I think it would be safe to say that most of us love to eat and treasure good food, a food empath is attuned to the energy of foods. Yes, food has energy, just like humans and animals, some more than others. When a food empath is absorbing so much energy from the world, he or she may be susceptible to overeating, especially foods that contain carbs and sugar. This most commonly occurs when they feel overwhelmed or highly stressed and anxious. A food empath is quite sensitive to the foods they take into their body.

  With increased awareness, an empath can control what foods are taken into the body and can eat in moderation and eat only those foods that are conducive to healthy nutrition.

- *Relationship and sexual empath:* These folks are attuned to their partners' and friends' moods, sensuality, and physical health. The closer you are to someone, the more intense empathy gets. To feel safe enough to let go in a relationship, it's crucial for empaths to learn how to set healthy boundaries and assert their needs. When this happens, real, authentic intimacy can occur.

Now that you've read about the various types of empaths, take the quiz in the next section and see where you are on the empath spectrum.

"TODAY I AM GOING TO SEE WHAT THERE IS TO SEE, TO FEEL WHAT THERE IS TO FEEL, AND TO KNOW WHAT THERE IS TO KNOW."
—BARBARA DE ANGELIS

Are You an Empath?

According to author Judith Orloff, M.D., Empaths are highly sensitive, intuitive, and caring, but they're also shock absorbers with an extremely permeable nervous system and hyperactive reflexes.

Empaths are highly sensitive beings who are sponges who absorb into their minds and bodies both positive and negative energies and vibrations from those around them.

As giving and caring as empaths are, they are prone to becoming overwhelmed, over-anxious and exhausted from absorbing too much energy from others. Empaths are the givers, volunteers, genuine, authentic, kind, sensual, great listeners, and can be great lovers. They also tend to over-extend themselves and end up energy depleted. Empaths need to replenish and rejuvenate by being alone. They tend to neglect their own self-care because they are giving it all away to others.

I work with many empath clients who don't understand why they are exhausted and anxious. Once we review the empath spectrum, they realize where they are and learn to embrace their gifts and challenges of being an empath.

If you are highly sensitive, intuitive, trusting, compassionate, nurturing, giving, and authentic, you most likely fall on the empath spectrum.

If you tend to absorb negative or anxiety-provoking emotions, you may be susceptible to physical symptoms including depression, anxiety, panic attacks, over-eating, increased alcohol consumption, exhaustion, chronic fatigue, and difficulty setting healthy boundaries.

If you are an empath, know that you have many gifts. Honor those gifts and respect your own needs. Find your balance and learn about practicing self-care and introspection. Embrace your challenges. Dive down to your heart center (center of unconditional love and power) from your head. There is an open portal on each side of your heart. Open one portal and go within. Keep breathing in relaxation and exhale through the portal on the other side of your heart. This promotes purpose, optimal health and well-being.

"WHEN YOU CHANGE THE WAY YOU LOOK AT THINGS, THE THINGS YOU LOOK AT CHANGE."
—WAYNE DYER

Learn to Embrace your Gifts and Challenges

I have heard science describe empaths as having a sensory processing disorder. Empaths are not disordered. They are gifted. Being an empath is a beautiful thing. As much as I have been wounded and hurt by others, I wouldn't trade being an empath for anything. It's who I am, and I love who I am. Empaths are also light workers, persons who want to serve humanity, and we need these people to stand in the light and save the planet. It is the empaths who will save this planet, not the narcissists. There is a concern that if we don't use our empathic skills, what will happen to our planet? What empaths could use some skill in is learning how not to take on and absorb others' energy.

About 85% of women and 15% of men are empaths; this imbalance may not surprise you. I may be speaking for many women when I say this, but I feel there is nothing more attractive and sexy than a man who is vulnerable, who knows who he is, and is oh so comfortable in his own skin without trying to impress anyone.

As mentioned, empaths have many gifts including the insight to tap into their intuition. They are sensitive, kind, caring, giving, loving, and the do-gooders in our world. Many have a radiance that gives off a vibrant energy from the soul. They automatically trust others and see the good in everyone. All of the above are the good points.

Sandra Brown, M.A., the author of *Women Who Love Psychopaths*, created the term "old soul empaths." She refers to these old soul empaths as having "super traits." There is a soul-to-soul recognition when you meet old soul empaths. Old souls are in all walks of life. Old souls are the ones who have and continue to believe, lifetime after lifetime, in the metaphysical, eastern philosophy, psychics, and mediums, and have a meditation practice.

According to Brown, old soul empaths are agreeable, conscientious, and self-directed. They generally have a great work ethic, are responsible and optimistic, have a can-do attitude, see the best in everyone, and are well put together…except when they hook up with a narcissist. Empaths are the ones who give 80% while the others give only 20%, if that. Empaths want to believe that everyone is the same as they are. Nothing is farther from the truth, and here's why:

- They believe that love can heal everything and anything.
- They don't realize that people can actually be predators.
- They believe that other people can and will change.

- They think they can help others change while they exhaust themselves.
- They don't want to give up because they believe in commitment.
- They see things through until the end.

One old soul empath, Dr. Brian Weiss, author of *Many Lives, Many Masters*, once said that in one of his lives he was persecuted for his beliefs. Those who are familiar with his work know that he is a Yale-trained psychiatrist, trained in western medicine. Dr. Weiss had a complete transformation in his personal and professional life when a patient under hypnosis described things about Dr. Weiss that no one would have known. In this life, Dr. Weiss has helped many patients and followers understand past lives and the healing that can take.

"AT ANY MOMENT YOU HAVE A CHOICE, THAT EITHER LEADS YOU CLOSER TO YOUR SPIRIT OR FURTHER AWAY FROM IT."
—THICH NHAT HANH

CHAPTER FOUR

THE EMPATH–NARCISSIST RELATIONSHIP

"PLEASE TO UNDERSTAND. I DID NOT CHOOSE TO BE BORN A VAMPIRE. IS UNFORTUNATE. I DO NOT HAVE MANY FRIENDS. BUT I MUST HAVE CERTAIN SMALL AMOUNT OF FRESH BLOOD EVERY NIGHT OR I WILL WRITHE IN TERRIBLE PAIN, LONGER THAN WITHOUT IT AND I CANNOT LIVE! PLEASE, I WILL BE DEEPLY HURT—I WILL DIE—IF YOU DO NOT ALLOW ME TO SUCK YOUR BLOOD...JUST A SMALL AMOUNT, MORE THAN A PINT I DO NOT NEED."
—RICHARD BACH, *ILLUSIONS*

With the information you have read thus far, you now know how empaths have a desire to help others and see the good in everyone. We are trusting and drawn to serve in every capacity we can for the greater good. Unfortunately, we have notoriously been targets for narcissists to prey upon. The can spot us a mile away. They seem to know just when to strike after they have targeted us to be their next victim. It is estimated that one out of every five people is a narcissist. I question that there are not more due to the covert narcissists that are so hidden and not found out until after the damage is done.

In this type of relationship, we don't even realize the depth of how we are taken, used, manipulated, controlled, and lied to until we begin to feel that something is "off," and we begin to lose ourselves by experiencing any of the following: feeling sad, anxious (walking on eggshells), or depressed; losing friendships because of absorption in the narcissist; fear of losing the narcissist if we don't do what he or she says; becoming physically ill (e.g., autoimmune disorder); or becoming addicted to alcohol or drugs. Remember that the narcissist wears the cloak of power and is a "master of darkness."

These energy drainers target those who are likely to put up with their tactics. Because they are so extremely masterful, they know what they are doing. They use and exploit for their own personal gain to the detriment of the empath. They use defense mechanisms such as projection on their victims or rationalization and justification, which are unconscious behaviors they are doing for themselves.

It's important to know that if you threaten to leave a narcissist, he or she will not change. They may say they will change; however, after they throw you a few crumbs to satisfy you, they will go right back to their old behaviors. Even if they tell you they are willing to see a therapist, it's rare they will go or stay long in therapy because they will either snow the therapist, if the therapist is not well versed in narcissistic abuse, or stop going because the therapist will call them out on their narcissism. No substantive behavior change ever emerges.

After years of neglect, the mental health profession is beginning to recognize personality traits and character disturbances these individuals have. We are now gaining an understanding of how to recognize these characters and learning protective strategies to take care of ourselves. We continue to gain an understanding of how to recognize and handle these impaired characters.

Recently, I watched the series about Ted Bundy on Netflix. It was fascinating to me because I remember him from the 1970s when I was attending Indiana State University and lived in a sorority quad. News spread quickly of the murders of sorority co-eds at Florida State University, and supposedly the murderer was still at large. It was still uncertain if the murders out west were connected. It was determined later that Bundy committed all of the murders. I remember a nervousness spreading at our sorority, and we were careful not to go outside alone at night, and made sure our doors stayed locked during the day, which was generally not the case.

As I watched this series, I was fascinated with how Bundy ended up in Aspen, where I now reside, and how he escaped jail and fled on foot to various areas nearby before he was recaptured. With my knowledge now that obviously I didn't have then, I saw very quickly Bundy's lack of empathy, manipulation, control, pathological lies, and charm, especially how he hooked in young women as he was on trial for murders of young women and acted in his own defense. Women were fascinated with him, and it didn't seem to matter that he was a cold-blooded murderer. That is just how conniving he was.

I'm convinced his good looks and charm had a lot to do with people having a hard time being convinced he could be a murderer. I did hear a couple comments from detectives referring to Bundy as a "psychopath, sociopath." Yet, even in the 1970s little was known about the criteria that help determine a psychopath. They are as high on the spectrum of narcissism as you can get. Bundy was convicted and lived on death row in a Florida prison until his execution by the electric chair. He confessed in the end as a manipulative tactic to get more time. It was clear that one thing Bundy feared was death. Although Bundy's mother claimed that he had a good upbringing, I question whether he was born a bad seed with something wrong with him from the beginning.

Cognitive Dissonance

When you are in a relationship with a narcissist, you will experience cognitive dissonance. *Cognitive dissonance* is a defense mechanism where one holds two conflicting feelings about the narcissist: 1) remembering the good times and the love for this person, and 2) taking on self-blame for the abuse and feeling that they are the crazy ones. You feel the trauma bond, the release of chemical cocktails that keep you bonded to your abuser and not even realizing you are going through this experience.

I remember this term being on my board examination. Little did I know how it would affect me in the future. The *New Oxford American Dictionary* defines cognitive dissonance as "Psychological conflict resulting from incongruous beliefs and attitudes held simultaneously. The state of having inconsistent thoughts, beliefs or attitudes, especially as relating to behavioral decisions and attitude change."

Now that I have lived to tell about my own experience with cognitive dissonance, I can understand the confusing aspects of this. I remember feeling frustrated at times due to the negative behaviors my husband displayed more often than not. I believed in the good in him, trusted him, never doubted when I married him that I would ever have to worry about major issues in the marriage that ultimately manifested.

I believed that he loved me, and these negative behaviors were such a contrast to my initial belief that he was a kind, genuine, trustworthy man of integrity. When you believe in something so strongly, it is so foreign when there is a contradiction. It's just unbelievable. Even now, after a few years, I still have trouble believing this happened, yet it did. I have kept the evidence of what I found in writing between him and his girlfriend at the time. I remember clearly conversations between he and I, and now more than then I see it all so crystal clear. I don't like and most likely never will like opening my eyes to the pain of what was. Even as I write this book, it still hurts.

Not that I would ever want to have any connection with him ever again. It's hard to explain. I tell others it was the loss of a dream. I still find myself saying, "How could he?" Yet the dissonance does remain because there were some good times. There were times he didn't put me down or criticize me in some form. Truthfully, however, as I reflect, there were not many times when devaluation didn't occur.

There is a saying that time heals. I believe it's what you do with the time that is healing. Some choose to get professional help and they learn various tools they can apply to healing. Others find ways on their own such as taking classes, writing, joining an organization, volunteering or all of the above. It's when one decides to rise above and move forward with life, healing can occur. When a past negative event does pop into my mind, I quickly shift to something pleasant, and then I begin to feel a calmness and know without a doubt that I am in control and free.

Dr. Judith Herman, who has studied trauma victims, found the most debilitating and chronic traumas occur when someone you put your trust in deliberately hurts you. Those who have experienced this horrific wound may not realize that the brain does not differentiate between physical, emotional, and psychic pain. Science has taught us with MRI studies that the brain registers life-threatening dangers from heartbreak and betrayal. A broken heart actually lights up the same brain centers as physical pain.

I have worked with clients who have died in their sleep of "natural causes." Yet I know from their life histories and continued betrayals, they died of a broken heart.

What Is Narcissistic Trauma Bonding?

When a narcissist is pursuing a partner, he or she showers that person with love and validation and love bombs them with flowers, champagne, gifts, trips, romantic dinners, affection, and adoration. You will be told how beautiful you are and how lucky he is to have found you. You may be told how you complete each other and an angel sent you. You get the picture. This may continue until you are "hooked." Once you are a submissive partner and the narcissist has control of you, the mask will begin to slide off; however, it becomes very difficult to leave because you are dependent on them and the relationship.

You start to trust that they are in love with you and will love you forever. You now depend on them for love and validation. You are bonded to them. The sex is good if not great. You completely trust them, and perhaps you are in love with them. You are dependent on them, and they know it. Now is the time for them to begin their criticisms, finding fault, perhaps even contacting their former lover, and there is always a former lover (or lovers) or spouse. Yet you trust that this is "the one" you have been waiting for, and you will be forever in love together through the remainder of your lives. You think future, building a family, or if you are older, you still think commitment, adoration, thinking this person will love you from this day forward. You are committed. Are they?

The narcissist gradually reduces the amount of love and validation that they give you and starts to criticize you and blame you for things. They become demanding. You will start to wonder why you can't seem to do anything right. The control intensifies. An example of this is if you want to have a night out and go to a movie with friends, you may be ignored, yelled at, told no, or given the silent treatment for days. This is the narcissist's way of punishing you and making you feel guilty for not including them in your outing. You see, because it's all about them, they will not see that maybe you want an evening out with your friends. Because the narcissist is so insecure, it's inconceivable that you wouldn't want to spend 24/7 with them. But sure thing, when you do go out, they will contact someone and let that person know you left them and will try and get sympathy as they play the victim. No matter how hard you try to make it right, they will make you feel like you did something wrong, when in fact, you did absolutely nothing wrong.

When the arguing beings, they tell you that this is all your fault. If you would only trust them and do exactly as they say, they would shower you with love again as they did during the love-bombing phase of the courtship. They try to make you doubt your own perceptions and accept their interpretation of reality. It's crazy-making behavior, and the narcissist wants you to begin to question your own sanity. It can be so subtle, yet incredibly dangerous. This is referred to as "gaslighting."

During this phase, you do not know what to believe, and at times you actually begin to believe that everything really is your fault. You think that your only chance of getting back the good feelings of when you first fell in love is to try doing things their way. They work at getting you to be submissive, because this gives them more control. Before you know it, they have you in the palm of their hand, and you become their puppet on a string. You begin to make more of an effort to try and please. You become co-dependent, meaning you begin to lose yourself and your partner becomes the priority, which is exactly what they want, because with the narcissist, it's all about wearing the cloak of power and control. It's also about winning.

As their control gets stronger, so does the victim's submission. When you try to fight back, they up their emotional and/or physical abuse. You pray for peace. You just want the fighting to cease because you are frightened and you don't want to lose him. This is want the narcissist wants. If you get a crumb, you will biochemically feel that there is hope, and the vicious cycle begins all over again (and again).

If your friends and family know, they are worried about you. You know that this situation is terrible, but you feel as if you cannot leave because this person is now everything to you. However, you may be closed mouthed and too embarrassed to share this with your friends and family. All you can think about is winning back this person's love, and how you can do it. You become obsessed. You are trauma bonded.

At this point in the partnership, you may ask yourself how it got this way. How did this awful relationship progress to the state of what it is now?

Remember, you trusted and believed in this person. They led you to believe you are meant to be together forever, until you were not. Yet your partner provides "intermittent reinforcement"; they will throw your crumbs, just enough to keep you in the loop of the abuse and toxicity of the relationship. The crumbs may include dinner out, flowers, a gift, an article of clothing, or the like. It's usually what they know you like and want so you will be so enamored of them for thinking of you, and the vicious cycle of abuse will repeat itself.

If you are going through any of the above trauma bonding, it is imperative that you get help to reprogram your nervous system so you can once again learn to self-regulate and get your life back. It is common for you to start to notice your pain ruling you. Don't be afraid to reach out to a trusted friend, contact a professional who is well trained in narcissistic abuse recovery, and practice self-soothing techniques such as a warm bath in Epsom salts, a massage, meditation, prayer, a spa day, a walk in nature, or being around an animal if you don't have one. Research has shown that pets are our true healers. I honestly don't know what I would have done without my close friends who I referred to as "My Team," my counselor, and my two dogs. Because of them, I always had someone to call when I needed to talk. I had my counselor on hand, who was always there for me when I needed him, and I had Annie and Archie by my side to comfort me. I was so blessed to have these resources. Don't ever be afraid to reach out, because it will help soothe your distress and bring you an inner strength you will need to carry you through to the other side, which is living life with truth, joy, and healing.

I have worked with clients who talked of obsessive thoughts about their partner. I, too, felt these thoughts. Time does help the thoughts fade. A few of the techniques I used with clients were hypnotherapy, the Emotional Freedom Technique (tapping), and eye movement desensitization and reprocessing (EMDR). I like these strategies because in hypnotherapy, we access the subconscious mind, which we operate from 90–95% of the time. Therefore, we are able to receive, absorb, retain, and accept the positive information being reprogrammed into the subconscious. We can also deprogram the negative impact of the betrayal. EMDR provides desensitization to the traumatic event. Through recalling a disturbing scene, the therapist uses a series of "sweeps" to desensitize the traumatic event, then links a positive cognition (i.e., how you would rather feel now), and repeats the sweeps until the client is no longer disturbed about the disturbing event. This is very effective and helps rewire the neural networks of the brain to feel healed. Remember that trauma does not 100% go away; however, EMDR can map the way to renewal.

I went through EMDR, and it was very effective for my own healing process. I also read, hiked, talked with friends, wrote, worked, and found all of these to be very productive distractions. This is all a part of the ever-haunting betrayal you experience. Remember that your pain is so intense that the preoccupation with your partner and reliving the scenes that are constantly replayed in your mind both aggravate and soothe your nervous system. Remember the cognitive dissonance? What we focus on expands, and with this preoccupation, it is no wonder we go through these obsessive thoughts.

Emotional Freedom Technique (EFT) is also known as tapping. This is a combination of ancient Chinese acupressure and holistic healing to physically alter your brain and your body's energy system. Tapping is known to effectively reduce stress and anxiety, and overcome depression, limiting beliefs, addictions, and specific fears. Tapping consists of using your fingertips on specific meridian points while applying a positive affirmation and talking through the specific emotional issues.

In Chapter Five, I will discuss how to expand ways of becoming resilient through the most difficult adversity.

Triangulation

Triangulation is a technique a skilled narcissist uses to try and make you feel less than or not good enough. This may be another subtle form of making you feel inadequate. In a triangulation, you will be the one to feel like the third wheel. Examples might be something like, "She's really going to have a hard time once we marry." "He's going to be my realtor. We're so close. You know, we've been friends for over twenty years." "She has come such a long way in her growth. I love being her spiritual counselor." See the putdowns? Making it seem as though you are not as important and the narcissist is God? She or he was a tool for the narcissist, like we all are. We are objects for the narcissist to feel powerful, in control, admired and adored, special, and most importantly, far better than you. Know that when a person is brought up in a conversation, there is always an agenda. They want you to feel beneath the person they are talking about and of course, feel beneath them. Their agenda is about putting you down to build themselves up.

Letting Go of a Narcissistic Relationship

As if it isn't difficult enough to have a breakup with a partner who is not a narcissist, there is nothing quite like breaking up with a narcissist. There is nothing normal about it. It's the way it is done, never without deceit, lies, manipulation, discarding, and devaluing you at your core essence. It's quite like nothing I have ever experienced before. For me, it wasn't just the fact that my husband was having an affair, it was the fact that he initially played stupid and asked me what an emotional affair was. But I think the worst was when he sat across a table from me and looked into my eyes with his hypnotic eyes and flat out lied. I gave him an out to fess up and come clean. He was not about to, and I really think that was the defining moment when I knew I was going to divorce him. He told me he was only seeing her professionally, which was an out-and-out lie because I had evidence through photographs on Facebook that they were together, and my close friend saw them at an event together, coming together and leaving together. He also lied about that. I just remember thinking, "This whole entire marriage was a lie, and I am not going to put up with any more lies." I'd had it. The betrayal had been done, and I had been traumatized, over and over. My source of security, trust, love, and joy had been thwarted. He had cut off what little he provided, and I was raw. I lived in fight or flight mode, never knowing what I could believe, and come to find out, it wasn't much. I don't ever remember a time when I felt so vulnerable. Although I didn't realize it then, I know now that I was in a neurochemical nightmare. It was normal to feel debilitating symptoms of PTSD. Again, I had not processed at the time that I was suffering from that. Somehow, by the grace of God, I knew I had to put myself in counseling as quickly as possible to rewire my traumatized brain and return to homeostasis. I did this as soon as I returned to Colorado after being in his presence in Florida. It's amazing how my body still gets queasy and that pit returns in my solar plexus when I think about it.

When I had made my decision to leave the marriage (which wasn't really a marriage), I felt it was necessary to go "no contact." I knew that if I responded to his erratic e-mails, I would be continuing the vicious cycle of submission while allowing him to wear the cloak of power.

I was not willing to endure his game any longer, so I blocked all lines of communication with him. Since I did not return his texts, e-mails, and any communication through anyone else he attempted to communicate through to get to me, his gas tank was empty. He had to continue to get the fuel he desperately needed for survival. Because he survived, it was clear that he had more than one source of supply for backup.

Again, I cannot emphasize enough that you need to get plenty of your own support, because you do go through withdrawal without your drug. You can find recovery programs in the resource guide at the end of this book. Much of inner recovery work includes healing your own abandonment wounds and working a program of healing where you can practice your own self-care and regulation.

I can see clearly now that the person I fell in love with was already damaged long before I knew him. This is true for you as well. This did not start yesterday. I also know that certain things I saw and loved in him initially were aspects of myself that he was reflecting back to me. I had no idea at that time, but after much inner reflection, I see that now. I have chosen to embrace what was and what I learned, and I realize what I learned a long time ago: if you don't take the risk, growth cannot occur. I have grown tremendously. My former husband will have to carry his suffering much longer than I did, because I chose to heal alone and do my work. He chose to line up other women and never even gave his own healing a thought. His loss. The lesson in all of this for me is that I was able to see in myself the qualities that I love that perhaps I would never have seen had I not gone through this. For that I am grateful.

I have devoted Chapter Six to individual interviews of people who have gone through betrayal and how they rose to resilience. These are people from all walks of life who have endured relationship hardship and had the inner strength to rise above. They will tell you it is a process, yet they did it, and so can you.

Withdrawal Symptoms

When you have made the painful decision to let go and leave the relationship, it is inevitable you will face withdrawal symptoms. This is much more than emotional.

As mentioned earlier, it is a biological fact that people in recovery from betrayal feel an addiction to their former partner. This is referred to as a biochemical trauma bond. There's a biochemical method to this madness. Recovery from an abusive relationship (physical, mental, emotional, financial, etc.) is akin to recovery from a drug addiction. This is because we develop a biochemical bond with our partner that is very difficult to break. The cognitive dissonance remains lurking in your brain; as mentioned, this is a defense mechanism whereby the victim sees two sides of the partner: one, the partner the victim loves and wants to be with, the false self; and two, the partner who abuses, condescends, manipulates, controls, and lies, the real partner behind the mask. Often the victim will deny, be oblivious, minimize, or rationalize the reality of what is occurring. This is a means of survival and coping with the predator. Because these biochemical bonds are so entrenched, it can be extremely difficult to leave a partner.

The withdrawal phase can last from months to years. Are you still in touch, or have you decided to completely go no contact? I understand if you have children, it is practically impossible to go no contact. If you can, please minimize your contact, because maintaining contact makes it more difficult to heal, and you are opening yourself up to additional hurt and pain.

We know the more you are in pain, the longer and more difficult it will be to heal. Being betrayed also brings on mental stress, and your system is now in fight or flight mode. Your hormones create a neurological cascade that strengthens your bond, which perpetuates trauma or betrayal bonding. This chemical phenomenon and the intermittent reinforcement that your partner provided creates confusion, and you begin to see him or her as someone who can alleviate your traumatized brain, especially because you still believe that your partner will relieve the actual pain that was inflicted on you. You begin to feel powerless over these biochemical reactions and feel as though you are withdrawing from a drug. You are, you are withdrawing from your partner. Your system is still in a state of shock, so you need help in reprogramming your nervous system. Your trauma gets locked in the central nervous system, and the destructive betrayal that has taken place is the deepest wounding of all.

Three Archetypal Wounds

Mario Martinez, M.D., has described three archetypal wounds: Shame, Abandonment and Betrayal. Many of us have these wounds from early on in our developmental years.

Dr. Martinez shares the corresponding "Healing Field" to each of these wounds. These are opposite energies from each wound that helps you shift these wounds to healing energies. If you have experienced shame, you can shift this to something honorable. Honor yourself and others. Invite others to share that honor with you.

If you have abandonment issues, the healing field is commitment. You stay committed to yourself and others. You remain loyal and don't abandon others. This will take you to your own level of evolvement and ultimate healing.

The healing field for betrayal is loyalty. Be loyal to yourself and others especially when they are in need. Now is the time to see yourself empowered, committed and loyal.

You don't ever have to internalize these wounds again. It's okay to give yourself permission to talk about them and begin to shed light on them. Remember that empaths are truly honorable, committed, and loyal. Show up in the room and be proud to be present for yourself from this moment forward.

Protecting Yourself and Your Children from Narcissistic Abuse

Whether you are divorcing, already divorced, or still in your relationship, if you have children, you will want to read this section because, now more than ever, if all of us can play some role in helping our children and youth so they can break the cycle of narcissistic abuse, we are doing our job. As M. Scott Peck wrote in his book *The Road Less Traveled*, "Life is difficult." I have worked with many adults who have suffered from this abuse, and now I am seeing adolescents who are telling me they are going through this tragedy in their families. This is difficult and challenging, yet there is hope and healing.

Although I do not have children of my own, I was a child of a narcissistic parent, and I remember all too well the shame, humiliation, and debilitating feelings I felt when I was around my father. I remember him acting as if he were embarrassed by the clothing I wore. From childhood, every time I visited him until my adulthood when I became estranged from him, he would say, "Are you going to wear that?," as if I had some horrible outfit on and he was ashamed to see me in public. Mind you, he didn't bother to purchase my clothing. I bought my own, and took pride in looking nice. Especially in adulthood, I dressed for success. I do remember the one time he complimented me on my outfit, only to turn and yell at the kind female server who brought our dinner too quickly. I wanted to walk out, but for some reason, I stayed seated full of shame and embarrassment that I didn't say anything. I had just graduated from college and I was still trying to please him. Being the child of a narcissist hurts.

There is no question that narcissism goes beyond self-absorption, lack of empathy, and greed. Children of one or more narcissistic parents grow up with no positive role model, because the narcissist is too self-absorbed to provide adequate parenting to the children. The spouse of the narcissist may have good intentions; however, there isn't a healthy emotional, physical, or spiritual relationship dynamic. Children raised in these families learn that it's about what they can do for the narcissist, not what the parents can do for them. This is a rough road to a co-dependent life with just about everyone, especially in intimate relationships. Co-dependency was a hot topic in the 1980s when I was getting started in the field of counseling and psychotherapy. When co-dependent, you are basically willing to give up or lose yourself for someone else. This is exactly what the narcissist wants you to do. It goes like this, "I'll do anything, just don't leave me." Children grow up with this feeling of inadequacy and not being good enough. By the time the child becomes an adult, there is an ever-present subconscious attraction to narcissists because this was not healed in childhood from having a narcissistic parent.

Because it's so unconscious, when the child becomes an adult, he or she unconsciously becomes enthralled with a narcissist to complete the love he or she never received as a child. We do not go into this with a conscious awareness. In other words, we don't say, "I'm going to select this partner because I need to work through the issues that I didn't work through with mom or dad." Chances are, until you are able to read some professional material or seek professional help, you will not completely understand these dynamics that play out in your own adult relationships. I didn't understand the dynamics myself as to why I was choosing narcissistic men until I sought my own therapy when I was 30 years old.

Here is what I learned about being raised by a narcissistic parent:

- I was always trying to please so I could earn the love of my parents, and it was daunting—especially with my biological father, because nothing was ever good enough.
- There was no empathy when I was searching for it.
- There was criticism and judgement.
- Emphasis was more on how one looks as opposed to how one is.
- Nothing was ever good enough.
- There was never any encouragement to become better.
- There were high expectations.
- There was envy, especially as I progressed educationally. I was not "college material." I was actually told that by both parents.
- There was no discussion of feelings.
- There was no understanding of self-expression.
- My father was an alcoholic and very critical and demeaning.
- There were no healthy outlets. I had to find my own.

These are some of the parent/child dynamics that continue to be handed down today in other families.

Although I was set up in many ways to be unsuccessful, I had the blessing and encouragement of my uncle who believed in me. Research shows that if a child has one healthy parent or caregiver, that child does go on to become successful in life. By successful, I mean many things—feelings of healthy self-esteem, belief in self, emotional honesty, motivation, desire, willingness to make the effort, loving what you do and doing what you love, and service. Not that this was easy, and it's still not easy. I just made the wise choice to rise to resilience with every challenge, failure, and lesson in this life.

It is my wish that our children, especially those who are children of narcissists, learn how to become resilient the way I did. I am living proof that you can rise to resilience no matter what circumstances unfold. Awareness does help prevent being sucked into a narcissistic relationship, and the more we can collaborate and increase awareness through knowing what signs to look for, the more we can use our own protection strategies and pay attention, tune in to our intuition, and lower the chances of repeating the cycle.

Help Your Children to Express Their Feelings

Some children are naturally expressive; however, if your child seems shy or overly sensitive, it's important as a caring and loving parent that you help them to identify and acknowledge their feelings. Often children repress their feelings for lack of knowing what to do with them or out of fear. Repressing feelings only leads to depression, addictive behaviors, and acting up in an unhealthy manner. The following strategies can help your children process and express their feelings for the greater good:

- Encourage your children to talk about their feelings. You can start by giving them examples of feelings such as happy, glad, sad, mad, frustrated, and joyful.
- Listen to your child's feelings, and let them know it's okay to express them by acknowledging and validating them.

- If your children are angry or frustrated, let them know it's good to release the anger by using a punching bag, punching a pillow, or participating in physical exercise. I also encourage my clients to write in a journal or on notebook paper, draw, or use art therapy to release their emotions.
- Accept their feelings, even though you might not agree. If they know you're a safe haven for them, they will learn the art of healthy expression and forge a path toward healthier development.
- I've noticed over time that children open up if you take them on an outing, such as going for a walk or ice cream. They develop more trust and feel safe revealing more.
- Although you may not always have the answer, that's okay. They may just need a hand to hold, a listening ear, and of course all the support you can give them.
- It's never too early to teach children how to meditate. Even if it is just for a minute, meditation is all about the breath and being in the here and now. If anything, they can learn to be calm and centered instead of worrying about what happened or is going to happen.
- By being an empathetic parent, you are sharing your heart with theirs. They will feel the connection and a sense of comfort knowing they are supported.
- It's okay if your children let their narcissistic parent know how they feel. If they seem frightened or have no sense of self, I would recommend you find a child therapist who specializes in narcissistic abuse and encourages healthy expression of feelings and healthy boundary setting.

These strategies can also minimize raising your own narcissistic and entitled children. You are the authority, and they need to know that. With your authoritative wisdom, you are being an appropriate role model for the ultimate healthy upbringing of your children. If you need assistance, you may try a parenting class and learn some additional strategies for bringing up healthy children. Even with a narcissist in the household, by healthy role modeling, your children can learn to be kind and compassionate, emulate good decision making, and be healthy functioning adults.

> "ACKNOWLEDGE YOURSELF FOR BEING CENTERED WHEN THERE IS INCREDIBLE CHAOS AROUND YOU. ACKNOWLEDGE YOURSELF FOR BEING COURAGEOUS AND DOING SO MUCH MORE THAN YOU THOUGHT YOU COULD."
>
> —LOUISE HAY

Strategies for Empaths to Protect Themselves and Heal from Narcissists

When you are feeling overwhelmed, overstimulated, exhausted, and low on energy, chances are you have been drained by an energy vampire. For your own self-care, it's important to take some time alone to rejuvenate and restore yourself. I tell my clients to take a mental health day and rest. Sometimes rest is the best remedy. Rest can center and ground you. This is necessary to regain your stamina. Balance is key in mind, body, spirit, and emotions. Take some time to use meditation throughout your day. Healing can occur in so many ways. Good will prevail.

The following strategies are also key in protecting yourself from energy drainers:

- **Set healthy boundaries.** If you know a particular person drains you, before you allow them to approach you via technology or in person, you have to know your limitations with this individual. A boundary is how far you choose to go with someone and how far you will allow that person to go with you. When I facilitate a hypnotherapy session with my clients, I do a body scan and use a protective golden sphere of light consisting of energy and warmth throughout the body to help relax all of the muscles, joints, bones, fiber, tissue, and so forth. Then I use this light to come back up around the entire body as a shield of protection against any external stress and pressure that comes their way. They exhale internal stress and pressure out into the gray mist and out into the ether. I tell the client the shield is always with them to protect from any negative forces. As soon as the client feels the presence of an energy vampire, they need to breathe, close their eyes (*not* while driving), and surround the body with the light that acts as a protective energy shield. The light can also be another color such as white or pinky violet, to name a few. I do this in public areas, especially at airports, crowded facilities (remember that empaths don't like crowds), and when someone is near me who I feel or know could drain my energy. It really works!

- **Stay away from narcissists.** This may be easier said than done, especially if you are living with or work with a narcissist. If you are, be aware so you can avoid their manipulation tactics. They can be subtle, so beware. I have counseled numerous clients who were faced with this dilemma. I know you don't want to risk your job, especially if the narcissist is your boss. In either situation, always use the shield to protect yourself, and you have to ask yourself if this situation is worth it to you to continue to endure being around someone like this. Do not allow your boss to devalue and degrade you. Your self-esteem is worth so much more. Get in a comfortable position and breathe. Do not let fear grip you. There are solutions. Keep meetings and encounters with your boss as brief as possible. With regard to a partnership, as you learn throughout this book, they do not change. All I can tell you is that there is life beyond living with a narcissist. There is a lot of support and, yes, you can leave. See my resource list at the end of the book. You can reach out to online communities for help and support, including counseling.

- **Ground and center yourself to the earth.** I encourage my clients to go outside and take their shoes off, when possible. (This can be a challenge if you live in a cold climate!) Hold your palms together and raise them above your head, and then slowly bring them down to your sides. Your feet should be about shoulder width apart when you do this exercise. Your feet will feel grounded to the earth, and that grounding becomes a rootedness that plants you solidly on Mother Earth. If it's cold outside, do the next best thing and just put your feet on the floor indoors. This exercise will give you inner strength from the bottoms of your feet to the crown of your head and all throughout your body. It's another protective healing strategy. Go out in nature whenever you can. Nature is healing. Use all of your senses and revel in the beauty that nature brings to us if we just spend time in it. Breathe in the fresh air, and hear the silence or the sounds of what nature brings to you. I don't think of myself as a moody person; however, there are times when I just need to escape. I always escape in nature, and after a couple of hours, I am totally with spirit and can return to the real world feeling so alive and nurtured by nature.

- **Perform a letting go ceremony.** A couple of months after I filed for divorce, I was visiting friends in Sedona. I knew I needed to go to a special vortex and have a ceremony to release my husband and the woman he was having an affair with. I drove to the place where I had been many times in years past. It was at dawn, and no one was there. I had a small flashlight, a smudge stick, matches, and a candle. I found the place and said a healing prayer and released both him and the woman and sent them on their journey. I also cut any cord I had remaining to him. I knew I needed to do this to totally and completely let go. Yes, they still come into my mind, but I just visualize myself free from him, and I already feel better. I flip the switch immediately, and I get instant relief. Releasing truly does free you of any energetic ties. It felt so healing, and I cannot tell you how cleansed I felt. A part of me knew that the affair wouldn't last because it was a sham as well. I found out their affair fell apart two weeks after I performed the ceremony.

  You don't have to visit Sedona's vortexes to perform a healing ceremony. You can do it in your own home. It is good to have a centering place to get started. Perhaps you want to create an area with some sage, a candle, maybe photos of a place you love, a special book, or something soothing. I have this on my nightstand.

Next, you establish a safe and sacred space. Begin with a meditation for a few minutes and get comfortable with setting your intention for healing. Put a beautiful healing light around your body. Ask that the negative energies and blockages be removed from your mind, body, and soul and be replaced with positive energies. You may want to send an energetic light energy to the person who has betrayed you. It's entirely up to you. Now just stay in this space and hold it until you begin to feel a shift within yourself. You can also energetically cut any cords remaining between you and the betrayer. You may then want to take a cleansing bath or shower or just relax and listen to soothing music.

- **Go and stay no contact.** Anyone who has been with a narcissist and has gone "cold turkey" (like I did) will find it is one of the hardest things they will ever do. The narcissist will try to suck you back in. He or she will continue to text, e-mail, use social media, and use whatever other means he or she can to win you back. Why? They cannot be with just one person, especially if their supply is running low. It's not that they want you; they want the idea of having you and others at the same time. They will say and do anything. Don't fall for it. It's pure manipulation. I can tell you that going no contact is an expedited way of healing and moving on with your life. It is empowering when you are in control and they can no longer control you.

- **Trust yourself.** You know that I am a huge proponent of trusting your intuition. Tap into your solar plexus, above the navel and your stomach region. I call it your inner guidance system. Your intuition doesn't lie. If you get a hunch about something or someone, it would behoove you to pay close attention. Probably one of the biggest lessons I had to learn was to trust myself again so I can trust others. I do tap into my intuition all the time now, and I pay attention. It's a beautiful gift.

- **Listen to music.** Listening to music is so soothing for your spirit. Sometimes when I write, I just have to have some music on. Mostly it's a nice instrumental sound, but there are times I play some rock n' roll and just jam to the rhythm. Music is therapeutic and a great healer.

- **Light and scent.** In addition to listening to music, I often light candles because they provide a nice ambiance and bring about a calm atmosphere. Even when I am reading, I have candles on and soft, light music. I love the feel of that. When I feel I have to release some negative energy, I will use a smudge stick. This is a Native American cultural tradition. Medicinal and aromatic plants will clear the negative energy. They remove the toxins and stagnant energy from a specific location. There are different scents of plants to use. It's really a personal preference. I tend to gravitate toward sage.

- **Have a partnership with yourself first.** It doesn't matter what anyone says about healing from a broken relationship—it takes time, often a long time. Again, everyone is individualized. I stress that everyone needs to develop a relationship with themselves first. Really get to know yourself—your attributes and frailties. Accept the you that has always been there, rain or shine, through thick and thin. When you feel healthy in mind, body, emotions, and spirit, you show up for you. When this occurs, you are returning to wholeness and oneness, a completeness that has been within you all along, though it tends to get lost along the way when you get off of your path. You deserve to love your path and its uniqueness, its many varieties—muddy, dry, snow covered with champagne sparkles, and wet and slippery. It's all a part of the journey as you come home to yourself and embrace what has always been there.

- **Be open to surrender.** Sometimes we try and hold onto problems we need to let go. This is where the act of surrender begins, and we make peace with ourselves. Surrender is the art of letting go. Surrendering removes obstacles to our trying to control out of fear. It actually feels good to let go and turn it over to a higher power. Sometimes I just look up into the day sky or night sky, hold my arms open, and turn it over. I say a prayer of gratitude and ask the Source to please take over. Surrender frees us up to be who we are without trying to be something we are not. It's very freeing to let go, and once you do, it's like emerging from a cocoon as a beautiful, free entity...a breath of fresh air. Ram Dass, author of *Be Here Now*, has a beautiful saying, "I surrender to my Intuition, to my wisdom, to my inner guru, and to the moment." It's so much easier than holding on, especially out of fear.

- **Keep your emotional centers (chakras) clear.** Chakras are the healing energy centers in our body, which have to do with energy flow. Chakras can be blocked, which can lead to difficulties on an emotional, physical, financial, spiritual, and mental level.

Cleansing and healing of chakras should be at the top of the list for optimal healing, because these energy centers in our bodies sustain health and lively energy for us. The following section discusses them in more detail.

The Chakras

There are seven chakras in the body aligned straight up and down along the spine. Each has a meaning and specific color affiliated with it. When we are operating at a high vibration, meaning we are empowered at a high level of consciousness. We are emulating clarity and a healthy outlook within ourselves. To specifically understand the chakras and their meaning, I will describe all seven chakras that reside in the body and their specific meanings.

1. Muladhara: the Root Chakra

   Color: Red

   Represents: Earth, groundedness, connection to Mother Earth, security, root, and base

   Muladhara is the root chakra of our body and is located at the base of the coccyx bone. It also promotes our instincts.
2. Svadhishthana: the Sacral Chakra

   Color: Orange

   Represents: Water

   Located in the pelvic region of the body, this chakra helps in the well-being of our sexuality, sensuality, self-expression, emotional connections, and interactions (including relationships), and the feminine expression.
3. Manipura: the Solar Plexus Chakra

Color: Yellow

Represents: Fire

This third chakra is located above the navel. It ensures self-worth, presence, responsibilities, power, and the intuitive essence within, including sensitivity.

4. Anahata: the Heart Chakra

   Color: Green

   Represents: Air

   The fourth chakra is located in the center of the chest and is known for unconditional love, the power center. It signifies love, devotion, compassion, and transformation. It also helps in the fulfillment of the gap between our lower and higher energies.

5. Vishuddha: The Throat Chakra

   Color: Blue

   Represents: The void

   This fifth chakra has the ability to speak truth in us and provides the gift of communication. It also signifies our spiritual awakening, power of communication, attentiveness, logic, and reason.

6. Ajna: The Third Eye

   Color: Indigo

   Represents: Tattva, an element or aspect of reality

   This sixth chakra is located between the brows and is known as the third eye. It signifies wisdom, divine consciousness, knowledge about sight and intuition, and inner vision.

7. Sahasrara: The Crown Chakra

   Color: White, violet, or no color

> The highest chakra, at the top of our head, symbolizes the crown, self-actualization, spirituality, and oneness with the divine.

In order to sustain optimal health and well-being, it is important to keep our chakras in balance. When we are faced with the day-to-day stress and energy drains of living, it is easy for our chakras to become unbalanced. Here are a few suggestions for chakra clearing and energy balancing:

- **Reiki:** This energetic healing is usually done by a Reiki master who places his or her hands on the area of the body that needs healing. The practitioner channels this energy, and blockages are removed.
- **Healing touch:** This technique is another energy-based approach to restore balance and harmony in the energy body on a mind, body, emotional, and spiritual level.
- **Craniosacral therapy:** This gentle healing modality is a hands-on therapy that stems from osteopathy, which is an approach that emphasizes the role of the musculoskeletal system. This wave-like rhythmic pulse flows through the entire body.
- **Hypnotherapy:** I refer to hypnotherapy as relaxed focus concentration. In a relaxed state, the subconscious mind is open to receive, retrieve, absorb, and accept suggestions that are mentioned for positive change.
- **Pranayama and breathing exercises:** Pranayama is known as the extension of breath. *Prana* is a Sanskrit word that means life force. *Ayama* refers to extend or stretch.

Pranayama is a yoga technique that uses breath work for many healing modalities.

- **Pranic healing:** This is a form of ancient energy medicine that uses prana, or life force energy, to balance and promote the body's energy.
- **Holistic medicines:** This is a form of healing that includes the whole person, body, mind, spirit, and emotions. Therapies are integrated to promote balance and wholeness.

Healing Chakra Techniques

Energy can become stuck in any of the chakras. When these blockages occur, there are ways to unblock the chakras and resume the flow of energy.

Healing of chakras should be addressed through the following:

- Root or base Chakra: stand bare foot on grass or sand and feel grounded and centered to the earth. Also a walk in nature can be helpful in clearing this chakra. The goal is to feel grounded and secure. Wear red and eat foods that are the color red.
- Sacral Chakra: This chakra is associated with creativity, sensuality and water. Take time to create, take a relaxing bath, or swim preferably in a lake or ocean. Wear orange and eat foods that are the color orange.
- Solar Plexus Chakra: This is the center of intuition and your inner guidance system. It is also known to be associated with the element of fire. You can get close to a bonfire or a fire place indoors. Wear yellow and eat foods that are the color yellow.
- Heart Chakra: This chakra is the power center and the center of unconditional love. Breath in love and take deep diaphragmatic

breaths and feel the air as you breath. Breath in relaxation and exhale heartache, heartbreak, and old wounds that no longer serve you. Wear the color green. Green is a healing color and eat foods that are the color green.

- Throat Chakra: This chakra gives you the ability to communicate effectively and speak your truth. To clear this chakra, sit in an open space (close to spirit) under the clear blue sky and get the energy flowing. Wear the color blue and eat foods that are the color blue.
- Third Eye Chakra: This is your wisdom center and it's associated with light. To balance this chakra, sit in the light allowing the sun to warm your body. Wear indigo clothing and eat foods that are the color indigo. An example would be blackberries and grapes.
- Crown Chakra: This is the center of the Divine. It is connected with the whole, including the previous chakras. The crown chakra is associated with the color violet. It is recommended that you spend time in meditation and contemplation. Nutrition encompasses all the previous foods. This chakra is nourished with spiritual practice. Wearing violet colors can be beneficial for you.

You can actually feel it when the chakras are cleared. Some of my favorite chakra clearings are through reiki and hypnotherapy.

"HUMAN BEINGS ARE JUST LIKE TEA BAGS....
YOU DON'T KNOW YOUR STRENGTH UNTIL
YOU ARE PUT IN HOT WATER."
— AUTHOR UNKNOWN (OFTEN ATTRIBUTED
TO ELEANOR ROOSEVELT)

Attracting a Healthy Partner

To attract a healthy partner, first and foremost you must have self-love. It may take many years, but it's never too late to have it. When you love yourself first, you have a much greater chance of attracting a healthy partner. I know that I always found the negative in me before any of the positive. It has taken a lot of work over many years (perhaps even lifetimes), but it has been so worth it. I no longer put up with any person who is not in alignment with what he says and his behavior. I don't need it, and I won't tolerate it, ever.

I now watch and listen for compassion, authenticity, genuineness, alignment, congruence, sense of humor, empathy, and laughter. I look for someone who knows who he is, is comfortable in his own skin, and asks questions as opposed to merely talking about himself.

The following are some questions to ask yourself—be brutally honest. (These are from a female perspective. Just change he/his to she/her if you're male.)

- Is he from a healthy family of origin?
- Does he tell his story with genuineness?
- Does he have integrity?
- Are his inner and outer selves aligned? (It doesn't take long to know.)
- Does he have friends, outside interests, and hobbies, and can he be alone and be comfortable?
- Does he share what his goals, dreams, and desires are?
- Does he want a long-term, sustaining partnership?
- Does he want a commitment?

- Is he honest and comfortable with sharing?
- Are his interests separate from yours?
- Do you have similar interests?
- Do you have commonalities? Do you know what they are? Are they enough?
- Is your time together balanced? Do you still maintain your separate friends?
- Do you sense integrity? Optimism? Kindness? Generosity? Passion? Love of self? Love of life?
- Does he seem to add to your growth with love, support, and encouragement?
- Is he there for you in difficult times?
- Is he genuinely nice?
- Does he add to your life on a soul level?
- Do your friends like him or see anything unusual or amiss that you've yet to pick up on?
- Is he willing to go slowly with physical intimacy so you can get to know each other emotionally?
- Do you listen to your intuition when you get a hunch, a thumbs up or a thumbs down, or do you discount it?
- After a period of dating, when the reality sets in, are you checking in with yourself on your own reality of how you feel about the situation?
- Have you felt angry over something said or unsaid, done or not done? Have you expressed your anger in a healthy and productive way, or did you repress it and shut down?
- Has your partner expressed his or her anger in a healthy and productive way, or was it repressed and shut down?

- Are you listening to what is happening in your body? Your body keeps score. If you get a pit in your solar plexus, pay attention because your intuition is trying to tell you something.

This is your checklist. Don't leave home without it, at least in your mind and heart.

It's not that I didn't look for these characteristics in my ex-husband; they were present in the beginning. If the person is not real, and you are paying close attention, you will know. Your intuition will tell you, loud and clear. Please pay attention and listen closely. Your heart is your best inner compass. My covert narcissist had many of these characteristics in the beginning, but I ignored them and the red flags, as you know from my story.

When there is conflict, and there will be, there needs to be a resolution. Do you and your partner know how to communicate effectively for resolution to occur? This is an integral part of the relationship succeeding. If one partner is not open to resolving the conflict and you are at an impasse, this creates little or no resolution and much unhappiness and mere existence. If there is an unwillingness to work together, there will be a repetitive theme and a vicious cycle with no resolution. When this occurs, it's best to move on and go your separate ways. You cannot move on without resolution.

When you are in conflict and you both realize that you want to resolve it, there is a strong likelihood for resolution and moving on together. For those who are dedicated to each other and are willing to compromise, learn, and grow together, anything can work. This demonstrates a genuine interest and concern on both parts to work through it together.

If you are dating a narcissist or someone who has the traits, even though they may not be a full-blown narcissist, please consider the potential consequences of becoming involved on a deeper level. Don't fall for their charm and manipulative ways. Note that you will never have real, genuine, authentic love. They are not capable of this. It's better to get out now than put yourself through the torture chamber of betrayal, the deepest wound of all.

If you have had the experience of dating someone diagnosed with NPD or you just know they have the traits on the spectrum, you will come to realize they were damaged, tortured souls before you knew them. People ask me how I fell in love with such a damaged individual. What I initially loved was not him; rather, what I loved in him were parts of myself that he was reflecting back. I had to work with my therapist to see the parts of myself that are my good qualities. Perhaps the relationship in the beginning was the closest I came to loving myself.

I know how very difficult it is to release the anger and hurt from your experience if you were with a narcissist. However, it is essential that you learn to clear your bitterness and all other negative emotions and choose to embrace the change this situation brought about in your life. I can honestly say that I have grown immensely from this experience, and I choose not to use the hurt I initially held onto in the beginning of the demise of the marriage.

I know that I am in a better place for living this chapter in my life, because I am not only surviving, but I am thriving now. I wouldn't wish the experience on my worst enemy; however, I know all too well that so many others are living it or have lived what I did. The best advice I can give is if you are in this type of relationship, get out and move on with the help of a professional who is trained in narcissistic abuse.

Chapter Five

Rising to Resilience

"There comes a time in your life, when you walk away from all the drama and people who create it. You surround yourself with people who make you laugh. Forget the bad and focus on the good. Love the people who treat you right, pray for the ones who do not. Life is too short to be anything but happy. Falling down is a part of life, getting back up is living."
— José N. Harris

The Journey to Resilience and Wholeness

Everyone is likely to experience hard times, even a traumatic event in their life—it is almost unavoidable. Everyone's experience of traumatic events will be different. How people are affected, cope, and recover varies greatly. We all know people who have faced great challenges and coped well with their stress while others seem to fall apart. What separates these groups? Resilience! It's the key to resisting stress, rebounding from it, and being your best. Our bodies have a natural tendency to be able to return to homeostasis.

Resilience means knowing how to cope in spite of setbacks, challenges, and limitations. It's about knowing your inner strength or using your spiritual muscles to rise to the occasion. Resilience is a measure of how much you want something and how much you are willing, and able, to overcome obstacles to get it.

Resilience is looking at difficulty as a challenge, not doom and gloom. Challenges present themselves as opportunities for growth, and people do just that when rising to resilience. They are able to view these challenges as solvable and not a reflection on their own self-esteem. They make commitments and stick with them in all areas of their lives—personal relationships, family, work, friendships, outside interests, and various causes they are involved in.

Resilience is taking control of a situation rather than feeling out of control. This helps them to feel empowered rather than powerless and paralyzed.

Leading psychologist Martin Seligman says the way that we explain setbacks to ourselves is also important. (He talks in terms of optimism and pessimism rather than resilience; however, the effect is essentially the same.) This "explanatory style" is made up of four main elements:

- **Permanence:** People who are optimistic (and therefore have more resilience) see the effects of bad events as temporary rather than permanent. For instance, they might say "My boss didn't like the work I did on that project," rather than "My boss never likes my work."
- **Pervasiveness:** Resilient people don't let setbacks or bad events affect other unrelated areas of their lives. For

instance, they would say "I'm not very good at this," rather than "I'm no good at anything."

- **Personalization:** People who have resilience don't blame themselves when bad events occur. Instead, they see other people, or the circumstances, as the cause. For instance, they might say "I didn't get the support I needed to finish that project successfully," rather than "I messed that project up because I can't do my job."
- **Personal control:** Resilient people spend their time and energy focusing on situations and events that they have control over. Because they put their efforts where they can have the most impact, they feel empowered and confident. Those who spend time worrying about uncontrollable events can often feel lost, helpless, and powerless to take action.

What do we know about resilient people?

- Resilient people have a positive image of the future; that is, they maintain a positive outlook and envision brighter days ahead.
- Resilient people have solid goals and a desire to achieve those goals.
- Resilient people are empathetic and compassionate; however, they don't waste time worrying about what others think of them. They maintain healthy relationships, but don't bow to peer pressure.
- Resilient people never think of themselves as victims. They focus their time and energy on changing the things that they have control over.

- Resilient people have internal strength and coping mechanisms that will help them triumph over adversity.
- Resilient people also maintain:
- A sense of autonomy (an appropriate sense of independence from family dysfunction, self-sufficiency, and a determination to be different—such as leaving an abusive situation and having goals to build a better life)
- Calm under pressure (the ability to regulate stress levels)
- A rational thought process
- Self-esteem
- Optimism
- Happiness and emotional intelligence
- A life filled with meaning and purpose
- Humor
- Altruism (learned helpfulness)
- Love and compassion
- Character (integrity and moral strength)
- Curiosity (which is related to focus and interested engagement)
- Balance (engagement in a wide range of activities, such as hobbies, educational pursuits, jobs, and social and cultural pastimes)
- Sociability and social competence (getting along, using bonding skills, being willing to seek out and commit to relationships, enjoying interdependence)
- Adaptability (having persistence, confidence, and flexibility; accepting what can't be controlled; using creative problem-solving skills and active coping strategies)
- Faith/spirituality in life

- Good health habits (getting sufficient sleep, proper nutrition, exercise, alcohol use in moderation, maintaining good personal appearance and hygiene, not using any tobacco)

Notice that resilience is a flexible, relative concept. It does not occur in an all-or-nothing fashion, but exists on a continuum.

The Path to Resilience: The Ability to "Leap Back" OR "Bounce Back"

Resilience is the ability to recover quickly from misfortune; to return to original form after being bent, compressed, or stretched out of shape. Humans are able to recover quickly from disruptive change or misfortune without being overwhelmed or acting in dysfunctional or harmful ways. Resilience is something we all have, but it takes courage, creativity, and strength. After a traumatic event, it is common for people to feel shame, embarrassment, and guilt. The fact that you survived should be celebrated and honored. Look at the ways you survive now. Are you present for yourself and for relationships? If not, it's common.

The reality is that we can survive and thrive from the experience. I am not trying to minimize the negative impact of trauma, but we can get incredible gifts. Positive things can come from trauma. We have the ability to gain so much insight and awareness that lead to growth.

Some thoughts on resilience from my clients:

- The ability to bounce back with new skills
- The strength to navigate tough situations, adapt, and function at a high level

- The capacity to absorb stress and maintain yourself
- Picking yourself back up and moving on
- The ability to improvise
- The acceptance of reality
- The belief that life is meaningful
- The ability to acknowledge the lessons learned and the wisdom within

Resilience can be cultivated. It's possible to strengthen your inner self and your belief in yourself, and to define yourself as capable and competent. It's possible to fortify your psyche. It's possible to develop a sense of mastery.

And it's definitely necessary to go back and reinterpret past events to find the strengths you have probably had within all along. Some evidence shows that it's not really until adulthood that people begin to surmount the difficulties of childhood and to rebuild their lives.

One problem is that there are elements of our culture that glorify frailty. There is a whole industry that would turn you into a victim and have you dwell on the traumas in your life. In reality, you have considerable capacity for strength, although you might not be wholly aware of it.

Sometimes it is easier to be a victim; talking about how other people make you do what you do removes the obligation to change. And sympathy can feel sweet; talk of resilience can make some feel that no one is really appreciating exactly how much they have suffered.

Resiliency is the capacity to rise above adversity—sometimes the terrible adversity of outright violence, molestation, or war—and forge lasting strengths in the struggle. It is the means by which children of troubled families are not immobilized by hardship but rebound from it, learn to protect themselves, and emerge as strong adults, able to lead gratifying lives.

Resilient people don't walk between the raindrops; they have scars to show for their experience. They struggle—but keep functioning anyway. Resilience is not the ability to escape unharmed. It is not about magic.

It's helpful to know the importance of resilience for a number of reasons: it enables us to develop mechanisms for protection against experiences that could be too highly sensitive and overwhelming; it helps us to maintain balance in our lives during difficult or stressful periods of time; and it can help shield us from developing deeper issues that we are unable to cope with.

A Resilience Action Plan

When I work with people who have suffered pain, grief, depression, anxiety, and trauma, I develop an action plan with them to help them begin to bounce back and lead to resilience. Some of these steps include:

- **Get enough sleep and rest.** Sleep deprivation is a real problem, especially for those who have been through challenging times. You may fall asleep from sheer exhaustion, only to find yourself waking up every half hour and tossing and turning until you finally fall back to sleep. This is a recipe for sleep deprivation and worry. We all know what it feels like to have to get through the day when we have not gotten enough rest, especially when this has gone on for weeks or even months. We might even try natural sleep remedies or medications that only have side effects. I recommend a glass of warm milk nightly, no computer or television two hours before bedtime, a couple of drops of lavender essential oil on your pillow, and even a lavender eye pillow. Lavender is calming and can aid in sleep. It's even helpful to listen to some quiet instrumental music or guided meditation.

- **Learn some self-soothing techniques.** These can range from an Epsom salt bath to taking time for a massage or an entire spa day. Light a candle, have some herbal tea, focus on diaphragmatic breathing, buy some fresh flowers, cuddle with your pet, ask for the magnificent energy of peace and possibility to flow through your mind, body, spirit, and emotions. Have a sense of compassion for yourself, appreciate what you have, and give gratitude.

- **Exercise your way.** I happen to live in an area that is full of world class athletes who train for many kinds of sports including the Olympics. I have struggled to think I am much of an athlete because I don't even begin to exercise like they do. I remember something my high school coach's wife once said, "Anyone who can walk is an athlete." Although I don't train for events, I do get out and walk every day, hike a few times a week, cycle in the summer months, and I belong to the local recreation center where I use weights. So my point is, any type of movement is a great way to feel good and take care of and nurture your physical body.

- **Practice cognitive restructuring to shift your negative thinking to positive.** Whenever a negative thought comes into your mind, say STOP, then shift that thought to something more pleasant and keep that thought in your awareness. There is no room for a negative thought because we become our thoughts. Focus on the positive because it's just as easy to focus on the positive as the negative, and you will have a much better outcome. Continue with the positive affirmations to keep the balance. Our brain is hard-wired to go to the negative. When you can reframe the current stressor, you are focusing in the present moment, just where you want to be.

- **Learn from your mistakes, and think of them as lessons as opposed to failures.** I often hear my clients say they feel they are a failure if they, for example, lost a job or went through a painful divorce. Perhaps instead of feeling like a failure, that could be shifted into a lesson learned, perhaps even an experience that one had to experience. Doesn't that have a nicer vibe? When one thinks along the lines of failure, that carries a low vibration and erodes one's self-esteem. Tell yourself that you have gained so much knowledge and learned a valuable lesson that does not warrant repeating. Repeat positive phrases to yourself such as "I'm a beautiful growing soul" or "the best is yet to come."

- **Embrace change.** In my most recent book, *The Gift of Change*, I mention that change is inevitable. As we embrace the many changes we go through in our lives, it helps to maintain perspective by acknowledging our situation, learning lessons from the choices we make, and moving forward to new adventures.

The Importance of Relationships

The ground-breaking resilience research of sociologist Emmy Werner, Ph.D., of the University of California, showed that about a third of kids never seemed to be affected by the grinding poverty, alcoholism, and abuse in the homes they grew up in. Of the remaining two-thirds, many were troubled as teens, typically turning to petty crime. But by the time they reached their 30s and 40s, they had pulled themselves together, determined to not repeat their parents' lives.

A troubled family can indeed inflict considerable harm on its children, but resilient people are challenged by such troubles to experiment and respond actively and creatively. The pre-emptive responses to adversity, repeated over time, become incorporated into their inner selves as lasting strengths.

To the degree that it is learned, resilience seems to develop out of the challenge to maintain self-esteem. Troubled families make their children feel powerless and bad about themselves. Resilience is the capacity for a person to maintain self-esteem despite the powerful influence of the parents.

The study demonstrated one of the cardinal findings of resilience research: those who lacked strong family support systems growing up sought and received help from others—a teacher, a neighbor, the parents of peers, or, eventually, a spouse. They were not afraid to talk about the hard times they were having to someone who cared for their well-being.

Relationships foster resilience. Resilient people do the active give-and-take work necessary to derive emotional gratification from others.

Reframing

Reframing is at the heart of resilience. It is a way of shifting focus from the cup half empty to the cup half full.

Cultivate resilience by thinking along three lines:

- **I Have:** Strong relationships, structure, rules at home, role models; these are external supports that are provided.
- **I Am:** A person who has hope and faith, cares about others, is proud of the self; these are inner strengths that can be developed.
- **I Can:** Communicate, solve problems, gauge the temperament of others, seek good relationships; these are all interpersonal and problem-solving skills that are acquired.

The Path to Forgiveness

When one has been betrayed, it can be very difficult to forgive. We go through grief, and one of the grief stages is anger. It's normal to feel anger toward the individual who hurt you. However, to carry that anger indefinitely is only hurting you. No, what was done by the betrayer was not fair; however, it was a part of a major life lesson for you to learn. If you carry this anger, it is as harmful for you as the betrayal was.

This really has to be up to each individual based on what he or she feels is the best solution at any given time. There may be a one-time occurrence that warrants forgiveness. There may be several acts where you caught your partner in lies; therefore, you feel this is not repairable. It's always good to attempt counseling, both individual and couples. If one partner makes excuses not to go to counseling, then one cannot do it for two, and you have to question why they are making excuses not to go. Most likely, they don't want to be called out on their wrongdoing or they simply don't want the relationship to continue.

Below are some questions to explore before making a decision on forgiveness. One piece of caution: If you choose not to forgive, you are only hurting yourself.

1. Is the person continuing this inappropriate and unacceptable behavior, or does he or she realize the hurt they have caused, and are they willing to change their behavior to be worthy of receiving your forgiveness?
2. Is that person deserving of forgiveness and even want the forgiveness? If so, the person needs to see the hurt and betrayal as wrong, admit it, and have every intention to not further engage in the behavior.
3. Did the person learn the lesson from this behavior, and is he or she willing to stop?
4. Do you know if this is a typical behavior or a first-time transgression? If you know this behavior occurred prior to you, it is likely it will happen again.
5. Has the person accepted responsibility? If the person takes no accountability, it most likely will recur.
6. Was the behavior malicious and intentional in order to hurt or punish you due to some action you took against them? (This doesn't necessarily mean you are aware of what that action is.)
7. What makes this relationship worthy of forgiveness?
8. Are you needing to forgive so that you can move on in your life? You can forgive (the other person does not even have to know because it is for you) and not maintain the relationship. This will help you to move on in a healthy manner.

There are no easy answers in terms of where you need to go with this. At some level, you have to work through the pain in order to move on with your life. This is very emotional, and I would suggest getting the assistance of a professional.

I also had a difficult time with forgiveness. While learning my life lesson, it occurred to me that although I struggled with forgiving him, I realized that he was the wounded and tortured soul. It was then I realized I could forgive him; however, I did not forgive his behavior. I separated him as a person from his unacceptable and inappropriate behavior. This was a very personal decision that seemed to work for me. I felt this was a compromise with myself that I could live with. I knew I would not be happy with myself if I failed to see the harm it would do me if I chose not to forgive at all.

I am not saying that this is a method that is cast in stone. Nor am I saying that it will work for you. You have to come to terms with the lengthy process forgiveness involves. Forgiveness does not happen overnight. It takes time to facilitate your own healing and make a conscious decision that you will go on and your life will be better. I felt that if I didn't forgive, my resentment would be a real blockage to my own growth and healing. I did not want to live day to day with ongoing resentment. It just felt toxic. I had had enough of toxic. I really wanted to release it. Once I was able to forgive, I felt a total freedom from anger and resentment. What happened, happened. It's over, and I have moved on. I feel happier than I've ever felt, I feel as though I have healed, and my heart has opened. I have let him go, I have let the marriage go, I have forgiven myself for ignoring the red poppies (flags). I, like many others, just wanted to be loved. Fifty-three years was a long time on this earth plane to wait to have love, marriage, and what I thought was an expansion and commitment in my life.

Forgiveness is very individualized. I cannot tell you what to do when it comes to forgiving your betrayer. All I know is that when I did my healing work, at some point, I was able to get to a place of forgiveness. This took time, and it was what I did with the time to heal and to let him go that allowed me to do so.

I also know that the man I was married to is also here to learn lessons, and I believe he has learned a lesson on what he has lost. However, all I know is how I feel, and it's a relief to forgive at some level, open my heart, and let go.

Allowing Love to Come In

When love involves a narcissistic partner, the end result can inevitably become dark.

There is nothing light about a pathological liar, a cheater, or being punished with silent treatments (passive-aggressive personality). You lived a part of your life with someone that you trusted and loved and expected that love and respect to be reciprocated. Their behavior was a calculated maneuver that left you with confusion, self-doubt, suspicion, and a pit in your solar plexus while walking on eggshells. Most likely you chose to stay longer than you could have by trying to make sense of it all.

If you have been through betrayal in a relationship or you are looking for love for the first time, to find real love, ideally you want to avoid getting involved with anyone who can't reciprocate your affections.

If you are in or have been in a toxic, abusive, nonreciprocal relationship, withdraw even when your passion is strong and tells you to stay, which it will. It may feel excruciating to let go when you don't want to or are afraid. If you're still hoping against all hope that the person will change, trust me, the heart knows when it's enough. I say, let your intuition and heart be your guide.

I want you to know that you have the ability to manifest authentic real love in your life whether you are 18 or 80. It's never too late to learn healthy tools for attracting the person who is somewhere on the planet wanting the same things that you want.

Now that you are beginning to become more resilient, you are naturally feeling a desire to learn how to allow love to come in. Bouncing back from hardship is not only possible, it's welcomed. Resilience is a skill that you can not only have and practice on a regular basis, but have in your life from now on, and you will experience deeper meaning of your purpose in this life. Resilience will provide a deeper meaning in your life because you are open to this stress-hardy ability to bounce back to be your very best.

Wherever you are in the healing process, as you learn to rise to resilience and re-create yourself, you will feel lighter, wiser, and happier, and you will achieve an inner peace that you have never had. If you want love, you will attract it because you are clear.

People ask me if it is best to spend time alone after a relationship breakup with a narcissist. Because of the wounds and possible PTSD, it is best to take time to heal these wounds because you don't want to be wounded while entering another relationship. If you were, what do you think would be the chances of it being healthy? Not great! So what does it take to heal and gain that momentum toward developing resilience?

Using Your Own Intuition to Pay Attention and Notice Who Is Unavailable

> "YOUR VISION WILL BECOME CLEAR ONLY WHEN YOU CAN LOOK INTO YOUR OWN HEART."
>
> —CARL JUNG

By learning these guidelines, you may dodge the bullet and escape the harrowing effects of falling for someone who is unavailable. It doesn't make it easy to ditch someone quickly, especially if you are attracted to them; however, if you notice the signs below in a potential partner, pay close attention to what is really going on.

- They are married or in a relationship with someone else.
- They can't commit to you or have feared commitment in past relationships.
- They have one foot on the gas pedal and one foot on the brake.
- They are emotionally distant, shut down, or can't deal with conflict.
- They're mainly interested in sex, not relating emotionally or spiritually.
- They are practicing alcoholics, sex addicts, or substance abusers.
- They prefer long-distance relationships, emails, or texting, or they don't introduce you to their friends or family.
- They are elusive, sneaky, or frequently working or tired, and they may disappear for periods of time.
- They are seductive with you but make empty promises.
- They are not in alignment with words and behavior.
- They are narcissistic, considering only themselves, not your needs.
- They throw you emotional crumbs or enticing hints of their potential to be loving, then withdraw.

Some of these signs may be more obvious than others at first. It's tricky: We tend to show our best selves in the honeymoon stage of a romance. It can take time for a person's unavailability to emerge. Also, we see only what we want to see. That's why it's eye opening to look at a partner's relationship history. Prior relationships reveal volumes about his or her capacity for a relationship now. Beware of rationalizing, "I'm different. This person would never be that way with me."

Most of us are not purposely drawn to unavailable people; it's very unconscious, and before we know it we are lured in. Also, unavailable people rarely choose to be that way. It's an unconscious defense against trauma or some emotional wound from that person's past.

The following suggestions will help you attract a healthy individual into your life:

1. **Set your intention.** Observe the persons behavior and check to see if it is in alignment with actions.
2. **Focus on the reality of the situation.** Does this person meet the criteria you have set? Be honest with yourself and refuse to settle for less.
3. **Take time to get to know the person.** You may have oxytocin (the love, bonding hormone) floating all around you, that is natural, however, you want to be practical and notice how this person is evolved in mind, body, spirit and emotions. Look at the whole person.
4. **Be aware of potential.** Be in the reality of the present moment. Do not fixate on this person's potential. Notice what is showing up in this person in the present moment.
5. **Notice the attentiveness and openness this person is giving to you.** Does this individual honor and respect you? Is there an authenticity? Is this person emotionally available?

This will help you determine if is worth your time and energy.

6. **Be prepared to let go if your intuition gives you a thumbs down.** You will be guided on this. It's a wonderful predictor.
7. **Love and honor yourself.** You deserve the absolute best. You deserve to be adored, treated respectfully, and treasured. Open your heart to this and you will bring in the love and kindness you deserve.

Healing Strategies for Stress Reduction and Building Resilience

"THERE'S A QUIET PLACE I KNOW WHERE NATURE SINGS TO ME THE MUSIC OF THE MOUNTAINS AND THE FOREST AND THE SEA. IT IS NOT FAR AWAY, AND IT SOMETIMES SEEMS A PLACE REMOVED FROM DAILY LIFE, A DISTANT DREAM OF TIME AND SPACE. I HAVE BEEN LOST IN CITY STREETS, IN TRAFFIC FAST AND LOUD, WHERE SIRENS SCREAM AND NATURE'S VOICE IS DROWNED OUT BY THE CROWD. AND SO I GO TO SEEK A PLACE WHERE I BECOME A PART OF NATURE'S SONG—THAT QUIET PLACE I'VE FOUND WITHIN MY HEART."
—PAUL CONRAD

I always tell my clients who are going through grief that healing takes time. What is most important is what you choose to do with your time. For today, stay in the present as much as you possibly can because the present will calm and center you. Try not to be out in the future because that can create anxiety. Yes, it's important to plan; however, when planning, be in the present moment. Stay grounded. I happen to believe that everyone grieves at their own individual pace, and there is no good, bad, right, or wrong way—it's your way.

Some days you may feel like you are doing well and you may even say to yourself, "I've got this." Then all of a sudden, the wave hits you and you fall apart. This is grief. If we can experience grief as learning to ride the wave, we will come to accept this is a part of the experience of healing. It doesn't make it a joyful experience, but if you can realize that you don't "get over it," you can still heal and come to an acceptance that grief is a part of life.

Sometimes my clients will be going through a divorce or they have survived the death of a loved one who had a major illness. They realize that they started the grieving process before the divorce or death was final. This is a rather common occurrence.

It's the same for someone who is healing from the depths of betrayal. For me, it helped to have a balance in my world in mind, body, spirit, and emotions in order to feel that I could come out of this and return to wholeness.

Mandala: A Symbol of Wholeness and Balance

All of the quadrants of the mandala (mind, body, spirit, and emotions) are connected, and to help you I will share with you what my personal mandala looked like as I sought ways to integrate these gifts into my life on a daily basis. The mandala continues to be quite helpful as I strive to show up and participate in all of these aspects to be the best I can be.

Most of us can say that we strive to reach wholeness and balance throughout our lives, even though at times we find ourselves getting off of our path. Being in balance and maintaining it can be challenging in all aspects of life.

My friend and colleague Brain Luke Seaward, Ph.D. taught me how to use the mandala in his holistic stress management course. The mandala figure represents a symbol of wholeness and balance, a way to restore natural equilibrium and return to each aspect of your true self. When we are out of balance, we feel off. So how do we regain that balance? It starts with realigning yourself in all of the quadrants—mind, body, emotions, and spirit—in terms of what you desire and how you choose to live your life on a daily basis.

To begin, draw your own circle on a piece of paper or poster board and divide it into four quadrants. Write your name in the center of the mandala, and label the four quadrants mind, body, emotions, spirit. These four quadrants compose your whole self. By using this mandala and working with each quadrant, you have a beautiful opportunity to restore yourself to that place of origin where you felt whole rather than what was programmed into you that became habitual over time. Start with the one that speaks to you initially.

It's important to know that you will find much of what you write in one quadrant will cross over into other quadrants as one easily connects to the other. That is fine. What you want to consider for each quadrant is the balance and harmony you want to achieve for your overall wellness and return to wholeness and balance, which is how you came into this world. You are a bright light, and through writing from your heart, that bright light is beginning to emerge from deep within.

Once you finish your mandala, find a place where you can view it on a regular basis as a reminder of your true self, the whole person you have always been. This mandala will be your guide to optimal health and well-being.

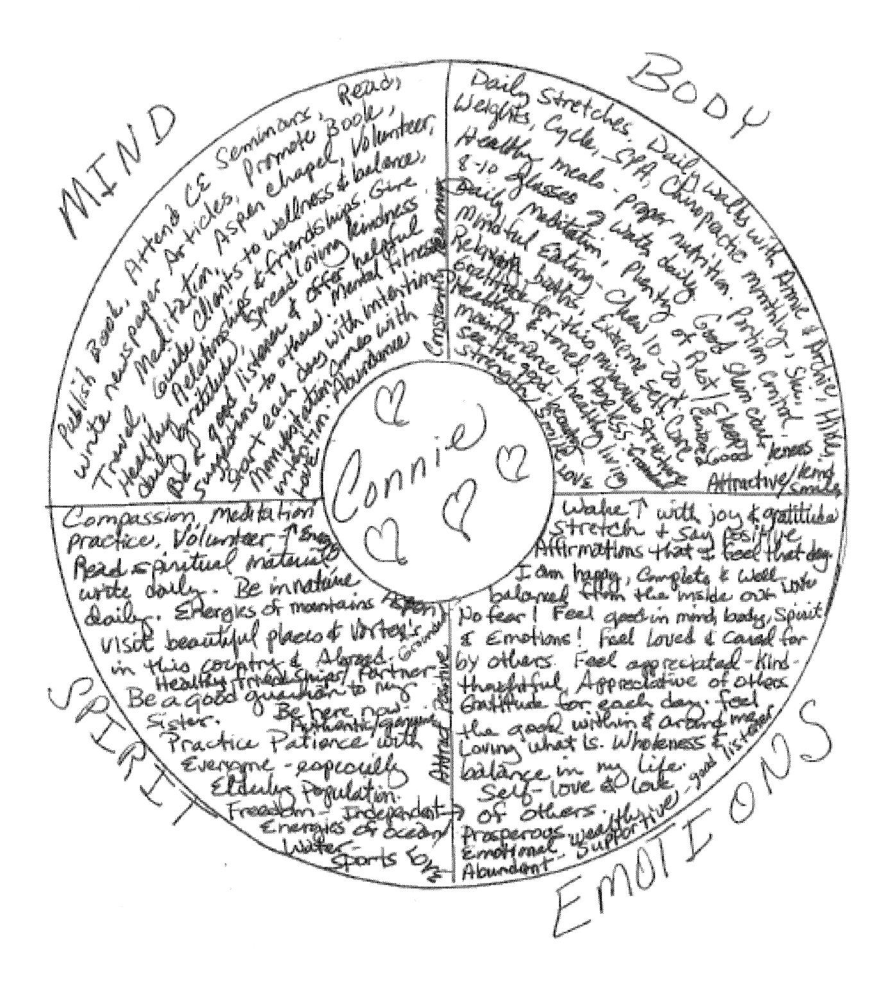

EVEN AFTER ALL THIS TIME THE SUN NEVER
SAYS TO THE EARTH YOU OWE ME.
LOOK WHAT HAPPENS WITH A LOVE LIKE THAT...
IT LIGHTS THE WHOLE WORLD.
—HAFIZ

Mind

I think of the mind as the intellect, that place where we think and use our left brain to be a part of the whole. There are many ways we can use our mind to achieve a fulfillment of this quadrant. Over the years, I have used my mind for education to complete the degrees I needed to practice counseling. I have read countless books in the areas of counseling theory and psychology and still have a yearning to learn all there is to learn about this fascinating subject.

My challenge was that while using my mind as a diversion, which was helpful, in many ways, I was also using it to obsess about the entire demise of my marriage. The incessant thoughts were enough to drive me over the edge! When the thoughts came in, I learned to visualize a beautiful scene in nature with my dogs who are my healers. I shifted any negativity and visualizations of them to a much more peaceful scene very quickly. I made myself do this to forget and desensitize myself from heartache as much as I possibly could.

As you use your mind, commit to thinking about what you really want as opposed to what you don't want. Remember that your thoughts are your mental energy, and you have the power to create your deepest desire.

I had an incredibly wise great uncle who raised me. He talked to me a lot about thoughts and what the mind can conceive. He would tell me that what the mind can conceive, you can achieve. That is the power we all have within us. It's up to us if we choose to use it.

My favorite author of all time is Dr. Wayne Dyer. For me, his wisdom and personality beamed beyond the moon and stars and back. I had the privilege of meeting him once following one of his talks and I said, "You are wonderful." He responded with, "And so are you."

Dr. Dyer spoke and wrote about how energy from the invisible field of spirit is perfectly balancing your in-the-world-calling with the pure energy of creation. He stated that what you are doing as you balance and align yourself with your dream is beginning to co-create your life. I can attest to this type of thought. For the most part, in my life I have been blessed with the ability to contemplate the life I acquired.

My eastern vedic astrologer tells me how he looks at alignments in my chart and that helps him chart my course. My thoughts are in alignment with my beliefs. Anytime they were not, circumstances were out of balance. Makes perfect sense.

Mindfulness-Based Stress Reduction

I have had an ongoing meditation practice since 2000. I attended a training on Mindfulness Based Stress Reduction (MBSR) at the Mount Madonna retreat center in California, facilitated by Jon Kabat-Zinn, Ph.D., and Saki Santorelli, Ed.D. It was one of the most insightful experiences I have had.

MBSR was life-changing not only for my career, but also for my personal life, for which I am beyond grateful. I continue to meditate on a daily basis. It may be for only a few minutes upon awakening, or a walking/hiking meditation, which lasts longer. Although I have been an optimistic and positive person throughout my life, I have also had anxious thoughts and needed something to help me relax and remain calm. I have gone on to teach Mindfulness Meditation classes, and it's one of my favorite teachings.

This type of meditation is a great reminder that when the thoughts come in, and they will, you simply return to the breath. That really resonated with me. There is something special about hanging out with yourself. Enjoy it, moment by moment.

Reading

I am an avid reader to begin with. When I needed to read and understand to a greater degree the spectrum of empaths and narcissists, I got my hands on and read every book I could on healing from this insidious type of abuse. I learned so much through all of the reading I did and felt that it was important to write my own personal story through a clinical mind. Parts of it were heart wrenching—to see in print what I had denied for a long time. Reading and learning was my new reality, and I had to go through my own process of healing to rise to my own resilience. Reading was painful, heartfelt, insightful, validating, and raw.

I also read humor and watched comedy for a break from the rawness of the narcissist, because that is heavy duty. Because of the work that I do, I have mostly read nonfiction books centered around psychology. My friends read a lot of novels and tell me how wonderful they are. Perhaps there will come a day when I am retired and will have more free time to take in some novels, but for now, I am content to continue my reading and writing to help myself and others continue on their healing path.

Compassion Meditation

Yes, there really is such a meditation practice as compassion meditation. A few years ago this meditation training was offered at the Aspen Chapel, where I attend worship services. I was interested in expanding my awareness, and it is always my desire to learn all I can take in.

The course was facilitated by Geshe Lobsang Negi, the director of Emory's Center for Collaborative and Contemplative Studies, where studies have shown test subjects who used this type of meditation had reductions in inflammation and distress in response to stressors, leading to an effective method for controlling high blood pressure. As Geshe explained, our western culture is just starting to learn more about practices designed specifically around compassion, which have been around for over a thousand years in Tibetan Buddhist monasteries.

Geshe shared that compassion is a skill we can learn. Compassion meditation helps to increase our empathy with others. We may want to begin with having compassion for a loved one, then move on to someone we have challenges with, and then eventually all the way to someone, such as a narcissist, who down deep is a tortured soul. Geshe goes on to explain how we can begin to see others with a common humanity and achieve common aspirations.

In the late 1960s, Dr. Herbert Benson of Harvard Medical School, a pioneer of the "relaxation response," conducted scientific studies to test the health benefits of meditation. In the "set point study," scientists found that each of us has a natural set point in our brains for both good and bad emotions. The study found that people accustomed to being happy have more activity in the front portion of their frontal lobes. There is evidence that for long-time meditators, the left prefrontal lobe of the brain adjusts the set point to higher levels. I naturally think of the monks who we mostly see smiling, such as the Dalai Lama. Research studies confirm that when one is living with inner peace and contentment, material possessions add very little to one's happiness. For those who practice compassion meditation, there are also known to be changes in the right hemisphere of the brain. These folks are found to have a higher sensitivity and emotional intelligence. They have the ability to efficiently manage and regulate their own thoughts and emotions. This, in turn, is most helpful in cultivating higher emotional states of joy and preventing depression in those who are prone to it.

Journaling

I kept a journal while going through a difficult and challenging time, and it was highly cathartic. The journal turned into the beginning of this book. I knew I needed to write. Writing has always been important to me. I kept journals throughout my schooling, starting in middle school. Writing allows you to explore deeply and go to those places your mind can shut off unless you allow yourself to dig deep. Journaling can be done in a simple spiral notebook or a special book that you purchase just for writing. It's fascinating to keep journals and re-read them years later and look at your life as it was and how it is now. It can be eye opening and very revealing into your true self. Some of my clients are afraid of journaling what they really feel for fear of being found out by someone in their household who may find it and read it. I suggest they find a place that is safe, or to have an actual safe for which only they know the combination. It's important not to deprive your mind of writing when journaling is such a cathartic way to use the mind, body, spirit, and emotions.

Travel

For me, travel is a beautiful journey into learning about and experiencing other cultures. I travel domestically to visit friends and family in Sanibel/Captiva, Florida, where I lived for many years. I also travel to conferences to learn more about ways to provide guidance for others. My profession is one of constant learning. I like to be involved in learning about all of the different and latest modalities to work effectively with others.

I also take international trips to learn more about other cultures. I travel to new places and meet up with friends, and also travel alone. There is something very empowering about traveling alone. I meet lovely people, both foreign and domestic. I love planning what to do and where to go, and I enjoy every step of the way. Sometimes I just wing it and spontaneously explore a city or town I didn't plan on visiting. I tend to love the smaller, laid back places. I find people to be friendly just about everywhere I go. I feel so fortunate to have had the wherewithal to just do it! There is such a sense of freedom in learning about other cultures and not really having a schedule.

I continue to plan trips and travel to new places internationally. I even have former clients whom I work with from all over the world and have been invited to spend time with them in their native land. It's such an honor to have this occur.

One of my most memorable domestic travel experiences was to Sedona, Arizona, in early May 2017. I was two months into filing for divorce. I took a road trip and stayed with some friends. Early one morning before the sun rose, I went to a vortex that I knew about and had visited for many years. I took a candle and a smudge stick, and sat on a rock that seemed to feel just right. I meditated for a time, then performed a ceremony to help with releasing him and moving on with my life. I knew at this powerful vortex something very powerful would occur. Within weeks of this releasing, I was informed that the affair he had been having with one of the women he was cheating with had ended.

I continue to travel because it is a passion, especially international travel. I probably will travel as long as I am able. I love using my mind for learning and growing. It certainly has helped me heal along the way.

These practices are a few of the ways we can exercise our mind.

Body

Our physical body is a miraculous structure that supports life from the cradle to the next dimension. It is my wish that we all honor and respect our bodies with proper nutrition, exercise, stretching, and love. I try and help women especially learn to love and accept their bodies for what they encompass. Rather than putting their bodies down and seeing every flaw imaginable, I work with them on recognizing every positive attribute until they are feeling worthy of their bodies as whole and beautiful.

In our culture, we are raised with the need to feel that we are supposed to have the perfect body that is slender, weighing and looking like the models on magazine covers. I am pleased to finally see a snippet of regular-sized women on the cover of a few magazines, and I am not referring to *Sports Illustrated* and *Vogue*. Far too many teens and women feel they are too fat, when in fact they are average size and weight. I cringe at the women who are living on an 8-ounce glass of tomato juice and a piece of celery daily to get that perfect weight for the next photo shoot. They are prone to osteoporosis, anorexia nervosa, bulimia, and diets that don't work due to starvation. Part of wholeness and balance is just that, balancing your body to eat the healthy foods it needs to maintain health and wellness. I pray our culture begins to wake up and realize that eating a whole food diet for lifestyle is the way to prevent stress and disease.

We do not have to be a super athlete to maintain a strong and healthy physical body. Some people simply don't like to exercise. I don't think you have to have a two-hour workout on a daily basis. I consider yoga, Pilates, swimming, and using weight training a great way to maintain health and fitness. Movement is exercise. I would recommend a balance of cardiovascular and anaerobic exercise for optimum conditioning. Exercise is about enjoying movement your way. Find something enjoyable in a time frame that works for you that brings you to a place of feeling your best.

Saying positive affirmations daily is a wonderful way to affirm a strong, healthy mind and body. An example of this is, "I love and respect every aspect of my body" or "My body is attractive, strong, and healthy." Even if you don't mean it initially, it can become affirming the more you say it and begin to believe this is true.

I have struggled with what I consider the optimal weight for myself over the years, despite the fact that I am quite active. I used to compare myself to thinner women and become so frustrated that I didn't feel I had a nice shape. It only made things worse. In my older and wiser years, I learned to let that go, as I am so blessed to be the epitome of great physical health. I am an avid year-round hiker, and I walk my dogs a couple of miles on a daily basis. I love to cycle in the summer, and I intend on maintaining my physical activity as long as my body is able. I am conscious of eating healthy foods, never drink sodas, and have an occasional glass of wine. I believe in moderation, so that means I don't deprive myself because I feel it can lead to binging. If I want chips or something sweet, I allow myself to have this in moderation. I don't believe in diets. Diets are something that you go on and go off. This can lead to binging and yo-yo dieting, which is extremely unhealthy for you, both physically and mentally. I hydrate and can get a full, satisfied feeling simply by drinking a lot of cool, clear, uncolored water. I have an average build, and I have to make myself do daily positive affirmations on my body being a beautiful, healthy, strong vehicle, which it is. I am blessed with great health, and I live in an environment where I can walk with nature and reap the beauty of hiking on many nearby trails to continue the strength of maintaining my strong healthy body. Just because I am not a tall, long-legged, model-like woman does not mean I don't have a fit, healthy body. It's all in our belief system and not the projections of what our society feels we should be.

It is my wish that the entire population of females learns to love and accept their bodies for all they can be and do. Then, and only then, can we live in a place of acceptance and grace.

Emotions

Our emotions are our feelings. There are far too many emotions to list under this heading. Our emotions can run deep from a simple happy, sad, glad, or angry, to a depth of emotion such as bewildered, confused, resilient, frustrated, shocked, and joyous from the depths of our soul. Just having an awareness of our emotions can also be thought of as our intuition, inner guidance system, inner voice, inner pilot light, self-realization, conscious awareness, inner soul calling, and a variety of other words. If we can learn to feel our emotions to the greatest degree, we are feeling the entire spectrum. There is a saying, "What we can feel, we can heal." We have to feel it first. At any given moment you have a choice, yet sometimes it's difficult to choose an emotion that makes you feel good. For instance, when we are in grief, we may choose anger, a very primitive emotion. It is one of the stages we feel when we are in grief, along with sadness, as I mentioned in the grief section in Chapter 2.

When one goes through hardship, it is easy to repress and deny the feelings we feel. We can develop hardened hearts and never feel that we can heal. When this happens, we just float through life and merely exist. It is when we can go for the gold, if you will, and get out of our head and into our heart that we really begin to feel what our heart wants us to feel. Once we can work through the difficult emotions that hurt brings us, wholeness and balance emerge.

I believe we are full of many emotions at any given time. The key is to be aware of our emotions and what they mean for us. I also believe that what we can feel, we are perfectly capable of healing—the hurts, disappointments, betrayals, abandonments, shame, guilt, and vulnerability that life may bring. There is something to be said about shedding tears as an emotion because this is a form of healing. It's also a wonderful expression of emotion to show joy and elation. It's contagious!

When we remember to rise above fear and embrace self-love, we can feel emotions that place us in a better position to thrive.

Spirit

When working with clients in this quadrant of the whole, I often see a puzzled look on their face. Some don't quite know what to write or even say. I tell them what the word *spirit* means to me, not that they will feel the same way. What resonates for me with spirit is mostly the energy of love. Just as to a musician, music is love, I feel spirit is with me all the time, through my ups and downs, good times and not so good times, and for me, that equates to love. I look at the word *spirit*, and I think in-spire, inspiration. What inspires me? What brings meaning and purpose to my life?

I believe that spirit is working within us and through us. It's not about our religious orientation, but rather evolvement of who we are as a species. I may not see spirit, yet I feel her presence.

Even though this may be the most challenging quadrant for many, it can be a remembrance of who you are. That's evolvement. I tell them that once they delve into pondering in this quadrant, it may mean something completely different for them. There is no judgment, just information that may give them a point of departure. I believe that we all have spirit as a commonality, some of us just don't realize it.

It's okay to take your time with this quadrant. You may need to dive deep into your heart before you begin and get into your feelings about the word itself, *spirit*. It's fine to jot down some notes, because you may find that nothing shows up initially. You may ask yourself, what is spirit, and what does it mean for me?

The key is to be able to eventually integrate these parts of ourselves into balance and wholeness so our lives can be the best we can be on all of these levels. When I explain all of these aspects of the whole in this way, the people with whom I am working seem to grasp that this is a major key to health, harmony, and wellness. Those who live and practice a spiritual life are able to discern what spirit means for them. For those who do not practice this way, they still can resonate, for the most part, that this aspect of themselves still is a part of the whole.

A New Partnership

Below are some tools to help you to listen to your inner voice when you are debating about bringing someone into your life as a partner. Let these resonate with you, moment by moment.

- I can create what I want and need from within. This person is an expansion of who I am.
- This person is in alignment with his or her words and actions.
- I can go within, love and heal any of these unhealed wounds myself, and not expect anyone else to heal them for me.

- I can only offer healing to myself from within myself; I can't heal anyone else.
- Whatever my potential partner offers me, I can enjoy expanding with him or her.
- I only have control over myself and my actions. I have no control over anyone, and no one has control over me.
- I am in alignment with my deepest self.
- Whenever I am faced with internal or external fear, I use the protective shield around me to keep the fear away.
- It is no longer about them. I am free from all narcissists, and I have developed and expanded my own healthiness.
- I am the strong and aligned true self. That's all that matters.
- I am a devoted light worker filled with light. There is no dark energy that can weaken me.
- I work on my trauma, healing one wound at a time, coming home to myself.
- I am grateful for the lessons I've learned and my evolvement. There are no mistakes.
- My breakdowns have evolved into breakthroughs. How fortunate am I?
- I'm empowered just being who I am.

From Dating 101 to Considering Commitment

After spending many years working with clients and seeing them repeat dating mistakes, I wanted to establish some dating guidelines to use as they enter the dating world and evolve into relationship.

1. Initial Date-keep it general. Do not share your life story with someone whom you are just getting to know. Focus

more on how you like each other; do you find your date interesting? Do there seem to be some commonalities? Are you noticing any red flags that would prevent you from going out again? Do you want to go out again?

It's perfectly alright to go on many first dates before you decide you want to see someone a second time. Remember healthy boundaries? It's okay to say no, which is a yes for you. If you are not interested in seeing this person again, simply let them know you enjoyed meeting them however you don't feel you are a match. Better to let them know up front than to drag it out when you are not interested.

2. Exploring A Second Date. You are interested in going out again. You are checking out compatibility and if you might want to begin seeing one another on a regular basis. You may ask if you feel a good connection? Do you have fun together? What do you like about this person? Is there anything that bothers you or have any red flags emerged since your first date?
3. Seeing One Another Regularly. Do you feel you are sexually compatible? Are there any issues that would get in the way of you continuing to see one another? i.e., long-distance, excessive travel for work. Are you comfortable sharing more intimate information with each other? Are you developing a sense of trust? Are you listening to your intuition? Are there any red flags yet?
4. Meeting Friends and Family. This adds another level to the relationship. Often this signifies the relationship is now exclusive. Do you like each other's friends and family? Is there a sense of comfort? Are you finding many differences now

as you continue to get to know each other? Are you paying close attention to any emerging issues that could cause you to deal with them together? How are you feeling about them? Has any issue emerged that you were able to resolve?

5. Considering Commitment. Are you at a point where you are making a commitment to this relationship? Are you on the same page with common goals? Have you asked yourself if you could be living with, married to, or you could see your partner being the parent of your children? Do you both want marriage and children? You are getting into some life issues that now go beyond just dating. Have you traveled together? Are you good travel companions if you have? Do you honor each other's alone time? What are your annoyances with your partner? Are you able to discuss them together? Are you still having fun? Is your relationship developing and growing the way you want it to? How do you resolve your disagreements? Are there any unanticipated issues arising that you don't know how to resolve?

It is imperative that you have on-going communication about the above if you are considering being together for the long run. If you have any doubt, then discuss your doubts and concerns. They will not disappear. The more you can eliminate issues that arise prior to making a commitment, the easier your relationship will be.

If you find yourselves encountering some problems and you find you are at an impasse, seek counseling together and work with a trained and licensed professional who can give you the guidance you need to take the next step.

Stress Management Strategies to Become Resilient

When you learn to manage your stress, you can rise above criticism, negative thoughts, concepts, and come to realize that no one has control over you. You are in control and empowered by your thoughts from within. With each positive thought comes positive energy that radiates through you. As you focus on the positive, you move away from stress and toward achieving your goals while accepting who you are. You will create balance and harmony when rising to resilience. You will build honor, appreciation and love for yourself. This will resonate with others and they will admire, honor and respect you.

The following strategies will enable resilience in your life:

1. Research shows that if we get out in nature two hours a week, our stress levels will reduce significantly. I know without a doubt this is true. I'm in nature at least one hour a day, and I don't know what I would do if I didn't have this. If it happens to be warm outside, take your shoes off and ground yourself to the earth. Feel the connection your body has and the centeredness you feel.
2. Cultivate resilience each day as you look in the mirror and say positive loving thoughts to yourself. Allow a moment to reflect your true authentic self and embrace the truth of who you are. When you treat yourself with the greatest level of success, others will notice your positive energy and it will radiate all around you. When you are resilient, you can send it out to others and help increase positivity. Nourishing our own minds and hearts primes us to love one another. Connect with your own resilience and wish your resilience

to grow and bless your life. Your resilience spreads an illumination that brightens the space for us all. Others will pick up on your energy. May your resilience be a collective practice. Each day you are getting better and better.

3. Choose love. This is compassion in action. We can cultivate love instead of fear. At any given time we have a choice to choose love. We are here on this earth for a fraction of eternity. Every moment counts. It is part of the journey. Remember what you focus on expands. So why wouldn't one choose love over fear? This moment allows you to re-awaken and allows you to choose. When you choose love you choose happiness.
4. Practice daily meditation. Even if you spend a few moments as you awaken each morning getting in touch with your breath, that is meditation. Cultivate present moment awareness as much as you possibly can. It keeps you grounded and centered and in the present.
5. Unplug. Take time away from electronics; news, social media, television, etc. Find some where to be quiet and take in the beauty that surrounds you. It's great if you can be somewhere in nature. Keep electronics outside of your bedroom at night and focus on the night sky and its beauty. You will sleep better.
6. Eat a healthy diet. You are what you eat. It is just as easy to eat healthy than not. Nurture your body with lots of greens, fruits, nuts and whole foods. Stay away from processed foods and be aware of your portion sizes. Drink at least 8-10 glasses of water a day and stay hydrated.
7. Laugh and smile at least several times a day. It's contagious. There is a person in my building at work who never smiles.

She just looks unhappy and miserable. I smile at her hoping that she will catch on and one day smile.

8. Get plenty of exercise your way. Find a way to enjoy movement. It can be a walk, swim, yoga, or being involved in a team sport. Just do it. You will feel good once you start reaping the benefits and you will.
9. Be creative. Take an art or music class. Learn a new skill. Ever wonder what it would be like to try something you have never tried before? This will add to your resiliency and it can even be fun.
10. Practice reading some comic relief. When you laugh, you loosen up your solar plexus muscles and it just feels good. It will raise your energy vibration which contributes to resiliency. As Dr. Judith Orloff writes, "Smile and Laugh more It will keep the energy vampires away."

Resiliency Exercises to Better Manage Your Stress

When I facilitate a hypnotherapy session, I tell the client that what the mind can conceive, you can achieve. That's the power of visualization. I also ask clients to see, feel, or imagine a beautiful golden sphere of light at the crown of the head, and we then proceed to do a body scan to relax the entire body. In the first exercise, you can do your own relaxation and body scan. Relaxation of the mind and body leads to resilience. The following exercises can help manage your stress levels and lead to feeling more resilient.

1. Picture a little ball of light-love dancing at the edges or bottoms of your feet. Pick a color, maybe it's golden, and allow

it to enter at the bottom of the feet, filling the body (body scan) as it moves through the body. Allow it to wash away anything that does not serve, letting yourself be loved and be love. Clear out anything that makes you feel small and does not serve you. Let yourself relax completely. Let the golden light shoot through the top of your head, feeling complete peace in this moment. The next five breaths will bring your awareness and attention back to the body. You have an awareness of other sounds...you become aware of awareness itself. Deepen the breath. Inhale from the belly, fill your chest and collarbones, and then exhale completely. Return to the body, and inhale and exhale completely.

2. Name the challenge you are struggling with. Observe your fear. Author Ram Dass wrote about inviting your fear in for tea. Let your fear know that it no longer serves you and you are ready to embrace your challenges and overcome them. This is resilience.
3. Keep a list of some accomplishments you are proud of. This can be simple; for example, "I showed up today," "I signed up to volunteer," "I painted a picture in my watercolor class." Give yourself a big pat on the back for your accomplishments no matter how small they may seem to you. Let your list be a reminder that as you continue to accomplish various tasks, you are rising to resilience.
4. Picture yourself getting into a hot air balloon, gondola, elevator, or helicopter—something to lift you up. What is it you are trying to do at this stage of your journey? What's important to you? See yourself rising up and letting go of

any negative thoughts. As you breathe in relaxation and exhale all negativity out into a gray mist that takes those thoughts out into the ethers, you begin accepting yourself more and more, which leads to resilience.

5. Close your eyes and think back to your 7-year-old self. Select a specific memory that was vibrant for you then, thinking of what his or her aspirations were for you. What did she or he hope for? From that place, what advice does he or she have for you now? Now that you have that token of wisdom, fast forward to your 90th birthday party. What do you see that is celebrating you at this time on the planet? What are the footprints you have left behind? Looking ahead now at this person, what advice do you have for her or him? Jot down anything that comes up.
6. What positive aspects of your life do you want to nurture? What parts of the new resilient you are showing up in you? As you move forward from this day, you know you want to nurture yourself and be your best self. Who are your champions, supporters that you can call upon along the way? What role do they play in your life now? What are you carrying forward from this day?

It Gets Better and Better

Life gets better. Believe me, it does. My clients look at me like I have two heads when I tell them that, in time, life does get better. We all want the magic fix. We want the pain to end yesterday. I wish there was magic dust to sweep away all the pain in an instant, yet it's necessary to go through it to come out on the other side. When we do, we can look back with lessons learned and smiles on our faces for having let go and moved on.

It is no secret that letting go and healing take time, and as I mentioned, everyone is very individualized in achieving this. For some, it's a month; for others, it is years. It depends on your coping skills and the degree to which you truly are ready to let go of the trauma.

I want to continue this chapter by providing other healing and coping techniques for you to have and use for yourself and/or through the help of a professional. Below are some of the healing modalities and healthy coping strategies I find to be very effective. Some of these coping techniques can be done on your own, while others require the help of a professional therapist who is trained specifically in this area.

1. **Eye Movement Desensitization and Reprocessing (EMDR):** EMDR is an interactive psychotherapy technique used to relieve psychological stress. It is an effective treatment for trauma and post-traumatic stress disorder (PTSD). We know that when a person is very upset, their brain cannot process information as it does ordinarily. One moment becomes "frozen in time," and remembering a trauma may feel as bad as going through it the first time because the images, sounds, smells, and feelings haven't changed. Such memories have a lasting negative effect that interferes with the way a person sees the world and the way they relate to other people.

EMDR seems to have a direct effect on the way that the brain processes information. Normal information processing is resumed, so following a successful EMDR session, a person no longer relives the images, sounds, and feelings when the event is brought to mind. You still remember what happened, but it is less upsetting. I learned in my

EMDR training that trauma never really goes away; however, through EMDR, a person can lessen the trauma to a significant degree.

Many types of therapy have similar goals. However, EMDR appears to be similar to what occurs naturally during dreaming or rapid eye movement (REM) sleep. Therefore, EMDR can be thought of as a physiologically based therapy that helps a person see disturbing material in a new and less distressing way. I have seen expedited healing through this type of treatment modality.

2. **EFT/Tapping:** Tapping, otherwise known as Emotional Freedom Techniques or EFT, is a combination of ancient Chinese acupressure and modern psychology. It is done by "tapping" on the meridian points of our body while saying certain statements. Clinical research studies have shown that tapping relieves chronic stress and pain, difficult emotional states, addictions, and PTSD. Tapping is known to have significant results in mind and body. The nine tapping points are as follows:

- Side of hand
- Either side of the brow and follow that bone down to the side of the eye, underneath the eye
- Under the nose
- The chin point—the crease between the lip and the chin
- Your collarbone—take your whole hand and stimulate the entire collarbone
- Underneath your armpit about a hand width from your armpit
- Your head—the end point

You begin by saying the setup statement: "Even though I have [a specific problem], I love and accept myself." Repeat this three times as you are tapping on your acupressure points. This is the first round. You are sending this calming point to your brain, letting your brain know you are safe, and while you are stimulating these pressure points, you are making a difference because you are giving your problem a voice. Being honest about how you are feeling helps to neutralize and remove any criticism and judgements.

Tapping can help you heal from grief and abuse, clear blockages to abundance and prosperity, and reduce your overall anxiety, worry, and negative emotions.

3. **Hypnotherapy:** Hypnotherapy, or simply put, relaxed focused concentration, is a great tool to access the subconscious mind. It is completely natural and involves diaphragmatic breathing, closing the eyes, and just allowing whatever happens to happen. There is no good, bad, right, or wrong way; hypnosis is your way. There are rapid induction techniques as well as more guided techniques that can include a body scan and some guided imagery.

The subconscious mind can receive, retain, absorb, and accept the post-hypnotic suggestions that the hypnotherapist is using to change the current conditions for the better. For example, if one wants to lose weight, I use a technique that is not about diet, but rather about lifestyle and eating sensibly. I have the subject eat breakfast, lunch, and dinner. I put out the suggestion to drink eight tall glasses of water daily, to limit alcohol intake if any, and that healthy snacking in between meals is fine.

We use the size of the fist as the portion size. I don't use deprivation because this only leads to binging. I say if you want something for dessert that is fine; however, you will only have a bite or two, and then you will get a full, satisfied feeling with no desire for more.

If the subconscious wants to take in the information, the positive change will be made. Hypnosis can be used for many healing modalities including setting goals and achieving them; weight loss; smoking cessation and other addictions; healing from betrayal, heartache, and abandonment; insomnia; and just about anything you want to change in your life. The power of suggestion can go a long way.

4. **Cognitive restructuring:** This is the ability to rethink your thoughts by changing your perception. This reframing, if you will, can help you change your perspective from what no longer serves you to resuming a new and renewed resilient life.

In our world of constant bombardment of stress and negative emotions, it's easy to focus on negativity. However, these negative thoughts only keep us stuck and prevent us from moving on to a healthy and vibrant new life. For example, instead of focusing on what is wrong, shift that focus onto what is right. Author Jon Kabat-Zinn, Ph.D., tells his meditation students that there is a lot more right with you than wrong. Before you go to sleep tonight, focus on all of the things in your day that felt good. You may just start with a few, but the more you focus on the good, the more the good will expand. We don't even realize how often we use negativisms without being aware of it. If you can become more aware, see how many negative self-talks you can convert to positive self-talks. Each day, your thoughts will shift to a more positive outlook—and there you have it, cognitive restructuring.

5. **Gratitude list:** Start writing down all of the things you are grateful for. If you prefer not to write them, then say them each morning when you awaken. I walk my dogs every morning and I am sure to look at the

mountains before me and give thanks out loud for everything that I'm grateful for each day. It's wonderful to feel such gratitude. It also sets the tone for the day to have more and more gratitude in your life, and when it goes out into the energy field it has a way of returning back to you. It's amazing how it works.

6. **Support systems:** When I interviewed the people in this book who rose to resilience from betrayal, one key element in their healing was having support. Support can come in many ways, from family, friends, clergy, professional counseling, books, YouTube, healing programs, support groups, colleagues, and even pets! If you don't have your own pets, shelters are always looking for people to walk dogs and visit cats. Who knows, maybe you will even adopt a loyal companion. It works.

I would recommend making a list of support people you can contact. Make sure these are people who replenish your energy rather than drain it. I had a list of friends and I called them "My Team." I knew I could e-mail, text, and pick up the phone (I did that a lot to vent), and someone was always there for me. I was beyond fortunate to have an amazing support team. You may want to make a list of your closest male and female friends. I loved having male friends during my healing, including a male counselor, because it was helpful to have support and perspective from men. It felt more balanced that way. It's also good to have friends that you can do activities with, someone to have a bite to eat with, go shopping, take a walk, share a gym workout, or even have a few friends over for a dinner party. It's a great distraction and uplifts your mood.

You can also meet new friends through groups or volunteering. Any type of involvement where you have an opportunity to make new friendships can be a healthy coping strategy.

7. **Hobbies:** It's good to have some hobbies and interests outside of your work environment. What do you enjoy? Is it a sport that you participate in, or is it more of a spectator sport? Is it playing a musical instrument? Photography? Perhaps you like doing some sort of art, writing, or becoming involved in organizations. I ask clients what their passions are, and often they associate passions with hobbies. Maybe you have thought about a hobby but have not explored it yet. I encourage you to put it into action and add this to your activities to feel a greater sense of balance.

8. **Forgiveness:** Although I wrote on this topic earlier in the chapter, I wanted to include forgiveness as a coping technique. Again, forgiveness takes time, and if you contemplate forgiving your betrayer, you can open your heart and learn to love and trust again. If not, this could be a major road block to finding love again. The choice is yours, and you will know in time what you want to do with it.

9. **Self-soothing techniques:** When you are grieving, and remember that grieving is healing, it's so vital to practice self-soothing techniques. It can be something that brings comfort to you. Some examples of self-soothing techniques are:

- Soak in an Epsom salt bath.
- Visit a hot spring and immerse yourself in mineral spring water.
- Drink a cup of hot herbal tea, no caffeine.
- Walk in nature.
- Get a massage.
- Read a book that you have been wanting to read.

- Cuddle with a pet or visit an animal shelter—animals are unconditional love.
- Be kind to yourself and say some daily affirmations.
- Get plenty of rest.
- Love yourself.

Ask yourself what spoke to you in this resilience chapter. These essential strategies were offered to help you in bouncing back from setbacks and trauma to cultivate your inner and outer resources to rise above and become resilient. The tools are designed to help with recovery from PTSD, anxiety, grief, and loss. Regardless of the obstacles that come your way, you will learn to thrive as you practice these techniques.

Becoming Whole and Balanced Heals Your Wounding

Your partner was a false self. There is no reason to be with or stay with a false self. When you become whole, you are healed and there is no way you can fall prey to a narcissist. You will see the signs no matter how slick they seem. There is simply no place for them in your life, ever. Narcissists don't seek out people who are whole. They only seek out those whom they know they can suck dry. They seek out partners who are wounded as well. Regardless of how successful, hardworking, and wonderful we are, if we have the slightest vulnerability, insecurities, and wounds that the narcissist can see and pick up on, we are toast.

Fortunately, with the resilience and healing strategies you have read thus far in this book, you are on the road to a full recovery, no longer needing to be the target for the narcissist's love bombing, discarding, devaluing, and hovering. You have some tools to help you pay attention and use your intuition before falling victim to them ever again.

You use practical skills when assessing potential narcissists, and remember to thoroughly watch their behavior to see if it's in alignment with their actions. You are now ready to discard anyone who does not meet your requirements of kindness and caring, honesty, and decency, first and foremost. You now have the wherewithal to take the necessary time to get to know someone before you see them as someone who can complete you. You pay close attention to what your inner guidance system is telling you before you act. You no longer will be manipulated and controlled, lied to and used. You trust yourself first. You are aligned with your true self. You are no longer susceptible to a narcissist. Congratulations!

Chapter Six

Individual Interviews on Betrayal and Resilience

I wanted to dedicate a chapter to those who have been betrayed and overcame their betrayal and carry the light of resilience. In my interviews, I met people from all walks of life—people who grew up in healthy families, and people who did not. The purpose of these interviews is to illustrate the striking similarities and common thread of their stories of being married to or in a relationship with a narcissist and how they healed their lives and rose to resilience. Their names have been changed to protect them.

Some of the women felt they became resilient over time, whereas others chose not to be in a relationship again because they felt they could not build trust. Understandable, and their conscious choice. The last thing anyone wants is to give one's power away to the person who harmed them.

These stories may inspire you to want to heal, live joyfully again, and have love in your life.

The interview questions consisted of the following:

- What attracted you to him in the beginning?
- What were the signs of his devaluing and discarding of you?
- How did your family of origin play a role?
- What was the final straw?
- What kept you from being the best you could be?
- How did you heal and rise to resilience?
- What is your life like now?

Client: N. W.K., Married 20 Years, Two Children

Therapist: What attracted you to him in the beginning?

Client: I was at the age I thought I should be getting married. He had a nice family, and he was handsome. I thought I was in love with him, and I believed in the institution of marriage.

Therapist: What were the signs of his devaluing and discarding of you?

Client: After my father died 10 years into the marriage, things started to crumble. We grew apart. My father would say that he could do anything, and my parents instilled working through the problems in marriage.

He was thin skinned. He couldn't handle anyone's sense of humor. The final straw was when she received an anonymous letter that he was having an affair. They had brief couples counseling, and she said he would rant and rave while she shut down. He said her family screwed him, and he accused her of reading all the time and not going to church. She felt that his affair made it easier for her to file for divorce.

Therapist: How did your family of origin play a role?

Client: His father and brother had an affair and stayed in the marriage and "worked it out." I knew I could take care of myself. I had a hugely supportive family. I didn't want to be with him, and I knew I was on my way out. When I confronted him, he said "Well, what did you expect?" He never apologized or took any responsibility for his actions. He played the victim card and projected his issues onto me. The entire marriage he was hardly ever home, and his son said as an adult that he realized his father was not there much. He was "saved" in the Baptist church. There were many silent treatments. I made an effort and tried to remedy. We had a lot of differences. He was very secretive and always made excuses why he wasn't home. The babysitter heard he was having an affair.

I worked full time and raised my children as he was gone a lot. When it was known that he had an affair, women came out of the woodwork and said that had happened to them.

My intuition told me I might get another chance at life, not even realizing it would be through divorce because he had affairs. I received a phone call from someone who was trying to piece together if he had an affair with his wife. I heard a lot about things he did with other women.

I believe it's better to want what you don't have than to have what you don't want.

Therapist: What kept you from being the best person you could be?

Client: My ex-husband.

Therapist: How did you heal and rise to resilience?

Client: I had a couple of bad relationships, and I didn't settle. I learned I didn't want to have something I didn't want. I also have a supportive family. They were supportive through it all. We are all very positive. That's our genetic makeup. I wanted to feel happy, and I knew that I had a choice. It's easy to be resilient when you have positive people around you. When you have kids, it's easier to cope with the betrayal. I cared about what would happen to my kids. He gambled with losing his family.

Therapist: What is your life like now?

Client: I have found love 20 years after my divorce. We come from similar backgrounds. He's flexible and will bend to make things work. I hoped I would have someone in my life and I would find love again. I thought I might meet someone who lost his wife. He was a widower. We were introduced through mutual friends. We are engaged now and planning a wedding for the fall. We're excited and very happy.

Note: The couple married and are living happily together.

Client G.B., Married 4.5 Years, No Children

Therapist: What attracted you to him in the beginning?

Client: He was an artist. I thought he was creative and interesting, not your typical NYC guy. I had an understanding and appreciation for what he did. I felt that we balanced each other.

Therapist: What were the signs of his devaluing and discarding of you?

Client: Halfway through the marriage there were red flags. I thought it was always my fault. We went on a camping trip, and he said here's what you can do to improve your image. He took no accountability and said he wasn't attracted to me physically. I felt that I needed to make this work and I'll make the effort.

He went from "this doesn't work," to "I think we need to get a divorce." I moved to Aspen, and he didn't move his things. I felt he was thinking, "I'll get her out of my hair and won't be bogged down, then I can convince her to have an open marriage." So we were back and forth, and I filed for divorce. He stalled. He wouldn't sign the paperwork. He played the victim card. My friends were caught in the middle. He said he wanted to stay married and live separate. He gave me an STD and I was furious. He took no accountability.

Therapist: What was the final straw?

Client: The May before I filed, I wanted to give it one more try. We went to Italy. I made all the arrangements. The second day of our bike trip we were biking to Assisi, and two to three miles up, he decided he wanted to climb faster, so I had momentum and we ended up passing each other. He was very competitive and he had to be first. This was supposed to be a trip for us to come together, and he's treating me terrible so I thought "screw it." I was going to put him on a train to Rome early, spend the rest of my trip alone, then go home and file for divorce. This was going on in my brain. He slept in the next morning and felt I was pushing him to get going. He adjusted my bike seat and I thought he tightened the seat. I thought to myself, in two more days I am done. We took off on a bumpy dirt road and I was standing, then I sat down and the entire bike fell sideways, and the bike seat fell off and before I knew it I was on the ground. He came over and said, "I can't believe you fell." He tried to pick a fight with me. He did re-assemble my bike, which was the nicest thing he did on the trip. I've never had a broken bone, so I thought I had a sprained wrist. When I pushed on the pack, I couldn't put pressure on my wrist. As we rode he was in front and I followed. He told me I had to go faster, and we ended up getting lost. He was leading and of course blaming me. By that time, my wrist doubled in size. He was mad and told me to keep going. I just held onto my bike in tears, in pain at the top of a hill. He was waiting for me, and at that point I couldn't use my hand at all. I ended up after my wrist dangled over the bars just walking the bike. I rode 25 miles with what I thought was a broken wrist, although he told me it wasn't broken. We checked into a room and I had ice for my wrist. We went out to dinner, and I just wanted to get my wrist taken care of.

The next day we went to the hospital 15 miles away. I came out with a plaster cast while he said, "I didn't think it was that bad. You killed a day and a half for me, and you need to pay me back." He didn't feel he should have to pay for that portion of the trip.

Turns out that when I returned to the states, I had to have surgery on my wrist. He lived near the hospital where I had surgery. I asked if I could stay at his place after surgery, and he came two hours after my surgery and said there was one problem, he had a date that night. He left me at his place, went on his date, and returned six hours later.

One year after the bike trip I was divorced.

Therapist: How did your family of origin play a role?

Client: My mother was the one who always took care of things for my father. As a wife, it was a domesticated female role. My father was good to my mother. You take care of things, fix things, and I ended up a caregiver, not realizing he took advantage of me. He had a dysfunctional background with lots of issues. He didn't have any good role models.

Therapist: What is your life like now?

Client: I have had a boyfriend for two and a half years. He helped me to be done with the divorce. We have been together ever since. I'm very happy, and I may even marry again. I would like it. There's not a bit of reason other than it allows for some things to be easier.

C.S., Married Seven Years, One Child

Therapist: What attracted you to him in the beginning?

Client: He was a father figure and 24 years older than me. He had financial stability, security, he knew how to be charming, and he was.

He was handsome, fit, and I fell for him. He proposed in seven weeks… he proposed marriage within two months of dating. After we dated for two months, I was pregnant. I knew his oldest daughter prior to the wedding. I learned about his youngest daughter four years after we were together. He denied she was his daughter, and I found out that he never paid child support, so there was a pattern.

Therapist: What were the signs of his devaluing and discarding of you?

Client: There were signs early on. One week after our wedding, I was a prisoner in our home. I would get dressed to see my family, and he would lock the door and wouldn't let me go. I couldn't go out with any girlfriends anymore. Part of this manipulated my mind to make me feel guilty. It became a cycle. He controlled how much I could eat. He would put food on my plate and tell me how much I could eat. He told me I was getting fat. He forced me to go to the gym. If I came home from work without my gym clothes on, because I often was exhausted from work, he would push me, call me names, call me lazy, and that is when the verbal abuse started. When he found out I was pregnant, he blew up. I was afraid of him. I broke down, and he asked me why I was crying, and it was because I was pregnant and I feared he would do exactly what he did. I always dreamed that my husband would hold me and be excited when I told him that I was pregnant. I had the complete opposite. He would explode, and it was so intense. Then came the honeymoon phase. The verbal abuse got to the point where I thought I was the worst human being on the planet. He wanted a boy, and when he found out it was a girl, he punched me in the stomach. My daughter was born with a birth defect called

Poland syndrome. I had her one year and two months after we were married.

Therapist: What was the final straw?

Client: The final straw was when I became suicidal. I was so brainwashed that I believed I was not meant to be in this world. He was right, I wasn't worth it. I put a knife to my wrist in the middle of the night. The angels came in and helped me to realize to let life take its course.

I filed for divorce. I did remarry him for the sole purpose to get my money back. I manipulated him in a healthy way. Six months later, I had breast cancer due to so much stress. I had a bilateral lumpectomy and a pulmonary embolism. I had complications, and it almost killed me. I had to have blood transfusions, and my body rejected the transfusions. The doctors told me that I may only make it another 20 days. That same day, I got a text from my husband's lover that they were having sex on our bed. I said out loud to myself, "God I will survive." Instead of them burying me, I will be out of this hospital alive, safe, and ready to file for divorce, again. I didn't get my money back after the first divorce, but I did get it back after the second one.

Therapist: How did your family of origin play a role?

Client: I missed having a father in life. My parents divorced when I was five years old. I missed my father. When I was little, he would caress my hair until I fell asleep. As an adult, when I would see my father, he would still caress my hair. I now do it with my daughter. So my ex took all of those things away from me.

Therapist: What kept you from being the best that you can be?

Client: My ex-husband.

Therapist: How did you heal and rise to resilience?

Client: Getting my money back in the second divorce and getting some freedom. Unfortunately, he never left me alone. He was arrested for domestic violence and arrested a second time for violating the protection order. It literally took me dying so I could learn how to be alive and fight for it. I have learned through all of these years to put myself first. I won't tolerate any more negativity in my life.

Therapist: What is your life like now?

Client: I am very happy, and I have someone in my life whom I adore and he treats me the way I deserve to be treated.

B.G., Married 10 Years, No Children, One Step-Daughter
Therapist: What attracted you to him in the beginning?

Client: He was very funny. He had a good sense of humor. We had a blind date and everything was elegant. He was physically attractive and British. I loved his accent. He impressed me. He was charming in so many ways. He had an aristocratic voice that he worked at. He had a beautiful apartment with oriental rugs, and it was beautifully decorated. He had the whole package it appeared. We were married six weeks later. I discovered after the fact that the whole thing was a hook.

Therapist: What were the signs of his devaluing and discarding of you?

Client: He was using my money. He didn't have any when we married and used excuses for not having money. He would threaten to return to England if I didn't give him money. He was nice to me, but he lied about everything. He was a pathological liar. When I first met him he was dating another woman and he said he broke it off. I found out after we were married that he never broke it off because she called when he was traveling and asked for him. I told her that we are married, and she said she has seen him and been with him. She said, "What we're dealing with is a liar." She also told me he married me so he could stay in the U.S. This happened a couple of months after we were married. He was in England with his mother at the time. I called him in England and told him we were done, finished and hung up on him. A half hour later he manipulated his mother and put her on the phone. She covered for her son. I relented and stayed with him for years. He totally drained me financially.

He was very grandiose. He was put in boarding school as a child, and his parents left him there on holidays. I think he made up a fantasy world because he thought he was royalty. We would go to a restaurant, and he said he was Lord Fairhaven and I was Lady Fairhaven. His parents were older and not there for him. There was an abandonment, and it really screwed him up. I confronted his mother about his lies and she confirmed they were just that, lies.

I had my own insurance company, and he had a travel business. I found out after he drained my bank account, took every dime, and my business went south. This was his way of getting total control. He isolated me and continued to lie, and I was still supporting him. Since I had no money, I had to come up with a scheme to get away from him. I got clever. I told him that I would be his sales rep if he paid for everything. He agreed, so I packed up and took my cats, rented a place in Florida as it was a status for his wife to be in Florida while he worked in another state.

The first time he visited me in Florida was a couple of months later. I played the game for as long as I could. I liked being without him, and I had an epiphany that I could never be with this man.

Therapist: What was the final straw?

Client: When he came to Florida we went for a beach walk as I loved the beach. He was hurrying me along and I had just had it. That night I told him I wanted a divorce, and he attempted to strangle me.

Then I discovered that he had been taking money from his customers in the travel business, pocketing it, then charging the credit card in my name. I had credit card companies chasing me, and I wasn't responsible nor did I know this was happening. He didn't pay his employment taxes. They came after me, then my attorney went after him, but I still had to pay a lot of the Amex bill. The whole thing was a nightmare. I filed for divorce and he fought it. Finally, after three years I was divorced.

He still pops up every once in awhile through emails. He was in the hospital once, and I got a call. His daughter has nothing to do with him. I have even received Christmas cards. He is a sociopath and has no regard for anyone. He only lasted in counseling a couple times, then never went back. All he did was lie anyway. I do think he loved me in his own twisted way.

Therapist: How did your family of origin play a role?

Client: I was close to my father, who never really cared for him. One time my father came to visit, and my father said something to him and he went off on my father and was horrible to him. I always felt bad that I didn't stick up for my father. After that, my father hated him.

Therapist: What kept you from being the best that you could be?

Client: I feared he would lash out and/or leave me. He could get nasty. He was a Jekyll/Hyde.

Therapist: How did you heal and rise to resilience?

Client: I got a part-time job and my family was so supportive and they helped me. I decided to get my real estate license and I stayed in Florida ever since. I made friends and I chose to have a great life.

Therapist: What is your life like now?

Client: I am a successful real estate agent, and I live in a beautiful home that I love and I created it all. I have wonderful friends and family, and I feel very content with my life.

R.B., Married for the Third Time, One Child from Previous Marriage

Therapist: What attracted you to him in the beginning?

Client: I wasn't attracted to him initially. He pursued me. I didn't know how to say no. Because of my dysfunctional childhood, anyone who paid attention to me was good, so I thought. I was willing to settle for anyone. We were married six weeks later. It was my third marriage.

Therapist: What were the signs of his devaluing and discarding of you?

Client: He never had any money and seemed to always be broke. He saw my vulnerability. The sex wasn't even good. I worked in the kitchen of a restaurant we owned, and I was exhausted after a very long day and I got down to 70 pounds and slept three hours a night. If I was too tired for sex, which I often was, he said I was frigid. When we finally started making money in the restaurant, he wanted total control.

He flirted with the servers in the restaurant. I got him a credit card, and we fought all the time anyhow. No matter how much I gave and whatever I did, it was never good enough.

When we had enough money, we bought a farm in another state and opened another restaurant. He isolated me and always had to be right. He was a horrible money manager.

Therapist: What was the final straw?

Client: When I found out that he was embezzling money from the restaurant. After this restaurant sold, he informed me he was moving to another state. I decided we would go together, even though he had several affairs that I knew about. Of course, he blamed me.

Then I confronted him about sexually abusing my daughter. He denied it and called us both horribly degrading names. He was into porn, and he made a list on a notebook of all the material things he thought belonged to him. He came into the marriage with nothing. It got to where we never saw one another. He was supposedly in meetings all the time. He also had a harem of young girls and thought he was a spiritual leader, a guru of some sort as he started wearing a white robe and a beanie hat. I was afraid of him and afraid to leave. He was so controlling that I didn't know if he might have me taken out. I had evidence he had those connections. We finally divorced, and it was the best decision I have ever made.

He ended up in jail for not paying child support, and I found out long after we were divorced that he was married a total of six times. I was his second. He passed away in 2019. I received a call from one of his ex-wives who knew. She told me the wives all commiserate.

Therapist: How did your family of origin play a role?

Client: I never knew my biological father. My mother was all consumed with my stepfather, who physically, sexually, and mentally abused me. How can anyone who has been through this come out with normal relationships with men? I married alcoholics, and my last was the narcissist.

Therapist: What kept you from being the best you could be?

Client: Never feeling that I was good enough. I had nothing but a series of toxic relationships that only brought heartache. I depended on men and all along I had the power to do it all on my own. I think that's the lesson.

Therapist: How did you heal and rise to resilience?

Client: I finally chose to be happy on my own. I've never been taken care of by a man. I just want to take care of myself and my beloved dog. I have a wonderful support system of women friends whom I cherish. I have been blessed to create my art, and it takes me to a whole other place. I don't have any drama in my life anymore, and I intend on keeping it that way.

Therapist: What is your life like now?

Client: It is peaceful. I live in a beautiful place and I feel content. I'm past the drama and feel healed. I just want to continue to do my art and live a peaceful life.

D.G., Married 18 Years, Second Marriage, One Daughter from a Previous Relationship

Therapist: What attracted you to him in the beginning?

Client: After a marriage and relationships that were unsuccessful, this husband sucked me in right away. My father had passed away, I was single, and I wanted to buy a house. I was a server, I had a baby, and I was going to school for a nursing degree, which I did get. I was proud of putting myself through school. He would come into the restaurant and tip me $100, and he would ask me out. Although he was still going through his divorce, he did spend a lot of time courting me. It was not a great physical connection, but I thought this might be good because I didn't feel the chemistry. He used my daughter to get to me.

The minute we were married, there was no calling me at work and asking me out to lunch, and he, along with the other men, put me on the shelf. There was a common theme with all of these relationships—they pursued me, hooked me, two married me, then put me on the shelf. This husband had money. Before were married, he wooed me. He took me on trips to great hotels, wined and dined me. He showered me with gifts, shopping, and money, all before we married. He was also an alcoholic.

Therapist: What were the signs of his devaluing and discarding you?

Client: He became sober, but didn't want to do the work. I taught him how to reestablish a relationship with his estranged children. His entire family was so dysfunctional. I did all the family entertaining and gatherings, but it didn't matter. I was not appreciated for all I did. I wanted to make the peace, and I gave away pieces of myself in order to maintain any sense of normalcy.

We also had an altercation and I was charged with domestic violence. I have been drinking on and off for years, and I am working hard at becoming a better person through my counseling and determining my worth.

Therapist: What was the final straw?

Client: His affair. He threw it in my face. He was so passive-aggressive. It just became so draining and so much work emotionally. I got silent treatments, and all I tried to do was be happy.

Therapist: How did your family of origin play a role?

Client: My father was an alcoholic. He was smart, and I love smart, intelligent men. I always wanted to marry someone who was intelligent. My first husband was good looking and intelligent but ended up being an alcoholic and physically abusive. After our honeymoon he left for three days and it was obvious his friends were more important than I was. He was drunk one night and held me hostage for four hours. I was finally able to get away. We divorced. He ended up committing suicide after having a pulmonary disease.

After my first husband, I met the man I had my daughter with. He was charming, and I was pregnant in less than a year. But he had already started to move on. He never supported our daughter. This guy was engaged to someone else and would spend the night with me. His bride to be didn't even know we were together. Then I married another alcoholic. I just didn't seem to be able to break the cycle. Looking back it's all so clear to me now. The one man I think I would have ended up with had a heart attack and died. He planned to divorce his wife and we were going to be together. I really think he was a good man.

Therapist: What kept you from being the best that you could be?

Client: The men I chose to have in my life. I kept repeating the pattern and attracted all narcissistic men. I have learned that alcoholics and narcissists are very destructive, and I was beaten down physically, mentally, emotionally, and spiritually. I had to work hard to get myself back, and this included being with yet another man after this marriage. He was a user, and I kept taking it. I spent a lot of money on him, and he continued to come back and still gaslighted me. He physically abused me, and I had to have surgery. His mother came and stayed by my side in the hospital. I know it was so I wouldn't press charges. I finally got him out of my life.

Therapist: How did you heal and rise to resilience?

Client: I didn't feel at all resilient after my first marriage. But I picked myself up and worked and went to school as a single mother. I also stopped drinking. After the last relationship, it took me moving to another state, and he still continued to contact me wanting money. It was the same old shit, and I finally realized this one is a total loser and would never change. I was his sugar mama. I never gave in to him again. He's the biggest regret of all the men. I'm just at the part of indifference now.

My resilience is bouncing back through my counseling. I am not dating. I've completely stopped, and I am content. If I am going to meet someone, it's because God wants me to. I want to go a year and not actively pursue dating. Last New Year I said that I need to wait a year. The most covert [underhanded and manipulative] one was the last husband. I learned a lot from all of these relationships. I know that I am now a better person, and I am healing.

Therapist: What is your life like now?

Client: I'm okay now. I'm tired of men, they are not worth the trouble. I'm taking time to work on myself. I enjoy my life now. I have my dog, I live in a beautiful place, have a great job, and feeling more resilient that I ever have.

Z.B., Married 11 Years, Two Children from a Previous Relationship

Therapist: What attracted you to him in the beginning?

Client: He was dependable, articulate, intelligent, interesting, and I was a single mother. I was attracted to his academia. He was quite the opposite of the edgy guys I previously dated.

Therapist: What were the signs of him devaluing and discarding you?

Client: He started responding to me in different ways. It was similar to the way he responded to his mother. He didn't like her. He wasn't respectful of my space. For instance, I would be cooking, and he would come home and drop his mail on the cutting board. He was the bread winner, and I was the stay at home housewife and mother. We had less to say to each other, and it was difficult with physical intimacy because I had a lot of issues with my hips. I have had surgeries and I was in pain. Instead of supporting me, he resented it, and so did I.

Therapist: What was the final straw?

Client: When I felt like I made a mistake. When 9/11 happened we were in New York. Since the planes were grounded, we had to rent a car and drive back to Colorado as we had two young children at home. Everything on the news was about 9/11. His immediate response was that America had to retaliate and kill. My response was that it would just perpetuate the violence. Right there he showed it's all ok until it hits too close to home. I discovered we had differences in our own value systems. Listening to him talk including his financial business, I thought I wouldn't want to be on the other side of him. I felt safe in the beginning, then I began to feel vulnerable.

He is the one who broke up with me. I was devastated. I thought he was into the family unit. I had small children and was surprised that he would break up our family. As I mentioned, I had ortho issues and it was hard for me to ambulate. In his mind, everything was a lot more disposable. After he moved out, we went on and off one and a half years before the divorce was final. After he moved out, I needed a spinal fusion and six months of rehab. The surgeon told me I would need my husband to help me. My husband told me he didn't give a shit what I needed and he wasn't paying for it. We had great insurance and had met our deductible. My 85-year-old mother ended up coming and caring for me.

I don't believe he had an affair before we broke up; however, as soon as we established custody of the children, I had them during the week, and he had them on the weekends, he started dating someone from out of town, and she was sleeping with him on the weekends in front of the children. We had done some counseling, and come to find out she suggested they return to counseling and he had gone on his own and the counselor gave him her blessing. I felt like I was sand bagged. He said she was the love of his life, and she had a son so he thought this was the new family. To his credit, their relationship continued for seven years. Eventually, she broke it off.

Therapist: How did your family of origin play a role?

Client: A lifetime of being vulnerable. I put up with things that I wouldn't have if I had a better self-esteem. I had no father present, and no sense that I was valuable. Obviously that carried over into my adulthood.

Therapist: What kept you from being the best you could be?

Client: My low self-esteem and vulnerability. I didn't have healthy role models.

Therapist: How did you heal and rise to resilience?

Client: I raised my children and developed a musical career under adverse conditions. I learned to play an instrument, and I made a conscious decision to have a career. I didn't have the energy at the time for a relationship. My children are now grown and doing well. They had two parents and continue to have a positive relationship with their father and myself. I wish they would reach out more, but I understand they have busy lives. I'm very proud of them, and they are their own people. The children were more important to their father than I was. I accepted that as I didn't believe I had value. I built my music career mid-life and was successful. It was quite an accomplishment.

Therapist: What is your life like now?

Client: I have a partner who worships and adores me. We have been together over a year, and I feel safe with him. Perhaps for the first time ever. We have great conversation, a lot of laughs, and we travel well together. We have fun. The main thing that helped me was regardless, I was not going to inflict myself into a situation that made me feel uncomfortable. That's where I am. For me, another big part of resilience is I've become aware of how everyone in my life was short-changed because I was short-changed. Others didn't get my best because I wasn't present. I'm working on forgiving myself for how it negatively affected my children. I know they don't feel that way about me. They have long-term relationships with people they've grown up with. They have better support systems than I ever had. I was an adequate parent, and that helps. I feel very blessed to have the life and resilience that I do now.

I am very grateful to these women who had the courage to share their stories. As you can see, they all worked through their betrayal and grief and learned to rise to resilience. Every one of them is thriving with their inner strengths and gifts, their creative spirits, and they all have a meaning and purpose in their lives. Wherever you are in your own healing, the common thread to these women's stories is they all not only survived, but now thrive, and you will, too.

Chapter Seven

Follow Your Dreams

If the chapters in this book have resonated with you, congratulations! You have most likely been through narcissistic abuse and you are on the road to recovery and healing. There is no doubt that you will think or even obsess about your ex-partner. This is natural. This is a part of your healing. You have so much to look forward to, and there is life after trauma. Your life will get better, and the best is yet to come.

Awaken with gratitude each day. Keep a gratitude journal and write about all that you are grateful for. This goes out into the energy field and it comes back tenfold. Set the intention that you can and will manifest what you want to bring into your new life. It's imperative that you remember to be kind and gentle with yourself and give yourself the time you need to heal.

This very moment, right here, right now, is all you have. The past no longer serves you. Part of your healing is letting go of the past and being as much in the here and now as possible. It will calm and center you. The present moment assists you with healing. Consider making proactive changes for balance and wholeness in your life. Review the mandala in Chapter 5 and use this tool to return to a more balanced and peaceful life. If you need the help of a professional, I encourage you to seek help.

Start thinking about your creative self, your talents, and begin to use these talents to your highest good. What do you love? What moves and motivates you? How do you serve? Focus on what you can change for the greater good for yourself and humanity. This helps with defining your purpose and meaning, the spirit quadrant of your mandala. When you are ready, consider volunteering because not only will you be giving to others, but you will also feel so much joy within yourself that you are serving others in a healthy, healing manner.

A part of my healing and recovery from narcissistic abuse, in addition to writing this book, was to get out into the community and volunteer. I wanted to focus on other things that could be helpful in my community. I have loved being a volunteer and writing to help others heal. It was important to me to transform darkness into light, and I have. One of the most meaningful volunteer positions that I have been involved with is the pet therapy program at our local hospital. The sparkle in the eyes of the patients when Archie walks into the room is priceless. What a beautiful way to give back. The unconditional love from animal to human. Now that's standing in the light.

Cease toxic relationships with others. You have survived narcissistic abuse and betrayal. Now learn to set healthy boundaries and end this vicious cycle once and for all.

You do not have to seek the approval of others, people please, or surround yourself with basement people—those who drag you down into their basement of negativity—any longer because you are coming into your own, regaining your energy, and becoming your best self. This is selfless. You are the priority. You no longer need others who don't accept or appreciate you for your own authentic self. If this happens to be a family member, try to decrease the time you spend interacting with this person and remember to set healthy boundaries. This means yes for you. There is only one unique you. Honor your true self, and you will get your life back.

Focus on and acknowledge your gifts and strengths. You do have them. If you related to embracing the empath's gifts and strengths and challenges, then use your empath gifts to share your stories and strengths with others. This is an excellent way for you to connect with other people who may need your expertise.

Use your sense of humor. Humor can lighten any darkness. If you don't feel that you have a sense of humor, then use laughter. Belly laughing loosens your solar plexus, your inner guidance system or intuition.

Be the light. Whenever I need protection, I ask for the golden sphere of light to surround me, and I know I am protected. Any outside external forces that come my way simply bounce off and away, and I stay safe. I am in the light, and I repel darkness. It's also a great way to move beyond being the victim and shifting into your creative self.

Who is your inspiration? It may be a leader, a relative, a teacher, or a friend. You can be your own inspiration and light because when you love yourself and stand in the light, you are the inspiration not only for yourself, but also for others. Others look up to you and are inspired by you. Imagine that you are the light for yourself and others.

If you can, take time for yourself and travel. Go somewhere you have always dreamed of going. Go with friends, a like-minded group, or explore on your own. It's such a wonderful sense of freedom and adventure. It's healing. There are so many beautiful places to explore in our world and such beauty to surround yourself with. I have been so fortunate to travel with friends and alone throughout my adult life. I made it a priority. There are still endless places I want to go, and I will go to as many as I can on my bucket list. I also found it very empowering to travel after my divorce. I concluded that I can do anything I want...well almost anything. I even went paragliding on my 62nd birthday!

In this life you deserve everything good that life has for you. Rise up from the depths of betrayal and live your best life ever. This life is but a fraction of eternity. Treasure every moment, for that is all we have. Love is available to us all. Be worthy of it because you are. Practice awareness, and be mindful of the nice and caring person who shows up and is available to you. Pay attention. Allow yourself to have courage, confidence, belief in yourself, and desire and expectation to let it in.

Love expands your life and takes you to a higher vibration. I know this. Just feeling love with friends and family, my animals, my career, and nature takes me to this vibration. I have no doubt that the unconditional faithful partner will show up exactly when he is supposed to show up, and my wonderful full life will expand, this time for the right reasons.

In the meantime, I have learned so much, and I thank all of those men I have been in relationships with because I have greater wisdom and love of myself, which has led me to greater evolvement. I am full of gratitude and peace.

I know when the next healthy partner shows up we will:

- Be best of friends
- Celebrate one another
- Continue to learn from each other and grow together
- Be open to life's changes and embrace them openly together
- Be trustworthy, honest, and not hold back or shut down

- Make our relationship the utmost priority
- Be open to say "I love you" and mean it
- Practice loving kindness
- Be open to speaking our truth without fear of judgement or criticism
- Continue to deepen our love
- Learn from our challenges
- Be each other's biggest support
- Give gratitude for each other each day
- Live with the excitement of discovering new things about each other and ourselves
- Embrace unlimited possibilities along our journey
- Reap the rewards of having found authentic unconditional love

It is my sincere wish for each of you to have this love in this lifetime. The potential to create everything you want is truly limitless.

ACKNOWLEDGEMENTS

My heartfelt thanks to all of you survivors and thrivers who chose to take charge of your lives and rise to resilience. You are the heroes. You had the courage to leave toxic relationships and heal. Many of you have shared your stories and interviews in this book. Thank you for your willingness to share. You continue to help others to thrive. You are my inspiration.

When I was going through my divorce, I was fortunate enough to have what I called "my team." I will never be able to thank you enough. All of you were there for me every step of the way, and did I ever need you. Annie, Brooke, Carol, Joan, Paula, Maryruth, Katie, Lee, Becky, Sunny, Renata, Luke, Moriah, Glenn, Jade: I truly don't know what I would have done without you. And thanks to the wonderful husbands and supporters who were behind the scenes support. You helped me above and beyond with your kind words and encouragement. You are the good men.

The folks at the Aspen Chapel who listened and were always there for support and encouragement. Thank you from the bottom of my heart. Greg, thank you for your amazing support and always being there. The wise women in my women's group who listened with empathy and support. Thank you.

A big thank you to my mom and stepdad, Joan and Ronn, you believed me and supported me from the start.

Every day and night, around the clock, I had pure unconditional love and comfort from my furry companions, Annie and Archie. How lucky am I? We cuddled, hiked, took trips, lived in several places, and through it all, you stayed by my side. Thank you my fur babies. I will treasure your love and loyalty for all of eternity. I love you both beyond words.

I am grateful to my clients. I learn so much from you. Thank you for your trust and confidence in me.

I am truly grateful to my editor, Toni Ackley. Thank you for perfecting my work with your good eye and helpful suggestions. You helped center me when I was all over the place.

To Anne Brown, Ph.D. Thank you for writing the Foreword to this book. Your grace and wisdom have been central to my life for twenty years. Your inner strength is beyond. You are true resilience and such an inspiration. Thank you for your guidance and all that you do to help others heal.

To my friend and amazing artist Lee Shapiro. Your goddess resurrection for my book cover is a beautiful entry into rising to resilience. We can all look to her and see the beauty within us. Thank you.

Thank you Brian Luke Seaward, Ph.D. and Marlane Miller for your kind endorsements. It means so much.

Educational Resources

I discovered when researching narcissism and betrayal, there is so much information, especially on narcissism. I read many books to gather as much research on the topic as I could. I learned so much, and I am grateful to all of the authors before me who taught me more than I knew when I began this writing journey. I want to pass along the resources that I used to help me write this book. I recommend the following books and websites for your own learning and healing.

Amen, Daniel G., *The Brain in Love.* New York: Three Rivers Press, 2007.

Amodeo, John, *Love and Betrayal: Trust in Intimate Relationships.* New York: Ballentine Books, 1994.

Anderson, Susan, *The Journey from Abandonment to Healing.* New York: Berkley Publishing Group, 2000

Arabi, Shahida, *Becoming the Narcissist's Nightmare: How to Devalue and Discard the Narcissist While Supplying Yourself.* New York: SCW Archer, 2016.

Ballard, Zari, *When Love Is a Lie. Narcissistic Partners and the Pathological Relationship Agenda.* San Bernardino, CA, 2013.

Borysenko, Joan, *It's Not the End of the World: Developing Resilience in Times of Change.* Carlsbad, CA, Hay House, 2009.

Brown, Anne, *Backbone Power: The Science of Saying No.*CA, CSF Publishing, 2013.

Brown, Sandra, *Women Who Love Psychopaths; Inside the Relationships of the Inevitable Harm with Psychopaths, Sociopaths and Narcissists.* Los Angeles, CA, Mask Publishing, 2018.

Burgo, Joseph, The Narcissist You Know: Defending Yourself Against Extreme Narcissists in an All-About-Me Age. New York: Touchstone, 2015.

Chodron, Pema, *When Things Fall Apart: Heart Advice for Difficult Times.* Boston, Shambhala, 1999.

Chodron, Pema, *The Places That Scare You: A Guide to Fearlessness in Difficult times.* Boston,

Shambhala, 2001.

Clancy, Constance, *The Gift of Change: Embracing Challenges Today for a Promising Tomorrow*. Bloomington, IN, Balboa Press, 2013.

Dennis, Sandra Lee, *Love and the Mystery of Betrayal: Recovering Your Trust and Faith After Trauma, Deception, and Loss of Love,* Sebastopol, CA, West County Press, 2014.

Durvasula, Ramani, *Should I Stay or Should I Go?: Surviving a Relationship with a Narcissist.* New York: Post Hill Press, 2015.

Epstein, Mark, *The Trauma of Everyday Life.* New York: Penguin Books, 2013.

Evans, Melanie Tonya, *You Can Thrive After Narcissistic Abuse.* Watkins Publishing Company, London, England, 2018.

Fuller, Tina, *It's My Turn: How to Gain Freedom from a Manipulating and Self-Centered Parent.* Amazon, 2013.

Jung, C.G., Staub, Violet De. Laszio, (Editor), *The Basic Writings of C.G. Jung.* New York: Random House, 1993. Originally published by Modern Library, 1959.

Kumar, Jay, Ph.D., *Science of a Happy Brain: Thriving I the Age of Anger, Anxiety, and Addiction.* Conneaut Lake, PA: Page Publishing, 2019.

Lesser, Elizabeth, *Broken Open: How Difficult Times Can Help Us Grow.* New York: Villard, 2004.

Love, Pat, *The Truth About Love.* New York: Fireside Publishing, 2001.

Luna, Alethia, and Mateo Sol, *Awakened Empath: The Ultimate Guide to Emotional, Psychological, and Spiritual Healing.* Create Space, Amazon, 2017.

Malkin, Craig, *Rethinking Narcissism.* New York: Harper Collins Publishing, 2015.

Martinez, Mario, Psy. D., *The Mind Body Code.* Boulder, CO: Sounds True. 2009.

McBride, Karyl, *Will I Ever be Free of You? How to Navigate a High-Conflict Divorce from a Narcissist and Heal Your Family.* New York: Atria Books, 2015.

Miller, Marlane, *Brainstyles: Change Your Life Without Changing Who You Are.* New York: Simon and Schuster, 1997.

Miller, Marlane, *Brainstyles for Lovers: Create Partnerships that Change Your Life Without Changing Who You Are.* Dallas, TX: Brown Books, 2004.

Mirza, Debbie, *The Covert Passive-Aggressive Narcissist.* Monument, CO: Debbie Mirza and Safe Place, 2017.

Northrup, Christiane, *Dodging Energy Vampires: An Empath's Guide to Evading Relationships that Drain You and Restoring Your Health and Power.* Carlsbad, CA, Hay House, 2018.

Orloff, Judith, *Emotional Freedom.* New York. Random House, 2009.

Orloff, Judith, *The Empath's Survival Guide: Life Strategies for Sensitive People.* Boulder, CO: Sounds True, 2017.

Orloff, Judith, *The Power of Surrender.* New York: Random House, 2014.

Ortner, Nick, *The Tapping Solution.* Carlsbad, CA, Hay House, 2013.

Pert, Candace, *Molecules of Emotion: Why You Feel the Way You Feel.* New York: Simon and Schuster, 2012.

Pert, Candace, *Your Body Is Your Subconscious Mind.* Boulder, CO, Sounds True, 2005.

Schiraldi, Glenn R., *The Resilience Workbook.* Oakland, CA: New Harbinger Press, 2017.

Seaward, Brian Luke, *Managing Stress: Principles and Strategies for Health and Well-Being*, 9th ed. Sudbury, MA: Jones and Bartlett Learning, 2018.

Seligman, Martin, *Authentic Happiness:* New York, NY: Simon and Schuster, 2004.

Simon Jr., George K., *Character Disturbance: The Phenomenon of Our Age.* Little Rock, AR: ParkHurst Brothers, 2011.

Simon Jr., George K., *In Sheep's Clothing: Understanding and Dealing with Manipulative People.* Little Rock, AR: ParkHurst Brothers, 2010.

Tolle, Eckhart. *The New Earth: Awakening Your Life's Purpose.* New York: Plume, 2006.

Van der Kolk, Bessel, *The Body Keeps Score: Brain, Mind, and Body in the Healing of Trauma.* New York: Penguin, 2014.

Webb, Jonice, with Musello, Christine, *Running on Empty: Overcome Your Childhood Emotional Neglect.* Morgan James Publishing, LLC, New York, 2014.

Useful Websites:

www.brainstyles.com

www.brianlukeseaward.com

www.melanietoniaevans.com

www.drjonicewebb.com

www.drnorthrup.com

www.drjudithorloff.com

www.selfcarehaven.org

www.afternarcissisticabuse.wordpress.com

www.healingfromcomplextraumaandptsd.com

About the Author

Dr. Constance Clancy is a holistic psychotherapist and hypnotherapist who has been practicing in southwest Florida and Aspen, Colorado, for thirty years. She received her degrees in education and counseling psychology from Indiana State University and Sam Houston State University. She received her doctorate at Nova Southeastern University.

Constance received post-doctoral studies in stress/anxiety reduction, hypnotherapy, healing from trauma (EMDR), betrayal, narcissistic abuse recovery, Mindfulness Based Stress Reduction (MBSR), embracing change, and finding peace after loss.

Using her considerable skills, Constance facilitates healing retreats throughout the country. She has also written weekly newspaper articles since the 1990s which are posted on her blog at www.drconstanceclancy.com. Her previous book, *The Gift of Change, Embracing Challenges Today for a Promising Tomorrow,* was published in 2013.

Her much anticipated current book, *In the Nick of Time: Rising to Resilience from the Depths of Betrayal,* was written to encourage those who have lived through betrayal to heal and become resilient by utilizing the tools for healing and recovery that she has prepared and used for many years in her counseling practice. Drawing on examples from her own life, beginning with betrayals in early childhood through her first and only marriage, she writes about how she overcame those betrayals to heal and become resilient, providing inspiration to her readers.

Constance loves to travel, especially internationally. While home in Old Snowmass, Colorado, she spends her time serving clients and hiking with her beloved Labrador retrievers, Annie and Archie.